expert • instant **expert** • instant **expert** • instant e

PAPERCRAFT

Joanne Sanderson, Emma Angel & Dorothy Wood

MQP

Contents

INTRODUCTION

Paper is a wonderful, almost magical material, sometimes as fragile as a flower, sometimes surprisingly strong. The more you experiment with it, trying out different papercrafts, the more you will learn about its exciting qualities, its many textures and colours. Soon every sheet will resonate with potential and merely picking it up will fill you with creative ideas.

Ordinary office papers and inexpensive card can be used for many papercraft projects, but if you want something really special you'll want to look at the fabulous handmade and hand-decorated papers available. So put down that cardstock, move away from your scrapbooking supplies and seek out stunning papers that speak your language. Choose papers layered with rose petals for feminine luxury or look for bold colours to evoke memories of childhood. Add glitter for glamour or explore the world of Japanese lace papers for a pretty, delicate touch. If you don't have a good supplier nearby then look on the Internet – there is a wealth of paper types out there, all potential papercraft masterpieces.

The projects and techniques in the book are specially designed to take basic cardmaking, scrapbooking and crafting skills to new heights. If you have woven background papers for a scrapbook before, then why not make a bag? If you are a fan of quilling, try rolling on a grand scale and make your own Christmas wreath. If you are a stitcher, don't stop at the cards – make a gorgeous corsage to wear on your favourite jacket.

Each chapter begins with a comprehensive guide to a particular skill – whether it is the correct way to cut out motifs for découpage, or the best way to make a fold for a card blank. You'll find plenty of tips along the way that will help you personalize your creations. So don't stop with the projects in this book – find some fabulous papers, get inspired and start creating gifts and cards to wow your friends and family.

Opposite: These stunning paper flowers are tinted with chalks and then coated with molten wax so that they float on the surface of a bowl of water.

part

1

THE HISTORY OF PAPER

PAPER MAKING IN HISTORY

Paper is totally indispensable for modern life, so it may come as no surprise that soon after the first type of paper was invented it became an important commodity whose manufacture and distribution was controlled by emperors and kings. Today's paper is based mainly on wood pulp but in the past it was made from anything from plant fibres to old fishing nets and cotton rags.

Paper has a fascinating if slightly confusing history because you could say that it was invented several times over, each time in a different form. With each invention either its base materials or the method of making it changed; but its main purpose remained the same – record keeping.

The word 'paper' derives from the Egyptian word 'papyrus', which was used to describe a type of paper made from the papyrus plant. Strips of the plant stem were cut, soaked, laid out together and then beaten to release natural starches. These starches formed a type of glue that held the beaten stems together. The word 'papyrus' means 'that which belongs to the house', or the bureaucracy of ancient Egypt, and indeed, at the time papyrus was regarded as so important that its manufacture was kept a state secret.

It is possible that papyrus was first used as long ago as 4000 BC but the earliest known example in existence is dated about 2600 BC. Just like paper today, it is thought that different grades of papyrus were made, and these were named after important officials. The Egyptians were also thought to recycle used papyrus for the mummification of bodies.

Chinese paper

Around AD 105 an official in the Chinese Imperial Court called Ts'ai-Lun invented a different type of paper, which is more like the paper we know of today. As an officer, Ts'ai-Lun's position gave him access to money and human resources, which enabled him to pursue his research. His version of paper was made of recyclable materials including bamboo, tree bark, hemp fibres, waste rags from the textile trade and nets from the fishing industry. His paper was less durable than papyrus but much cheaper and easier to make, and it made him a wealthy man. As with papyrus, the techniques for making this new paper were kept secret.

Arab version

As with all good inventions, the secret of paper-making had to get out some time, and around AD 750 some Chinese paper manufacturers were captured by Arabs and gave up their secrets. The method of making paper also

Left: Laid paper being made in a small handmade paper shop in Amalfi, Italy, using paper pulp and a wire frame called a 'deckle'.
Opposite: Pressing and hanging paper, ca. 1700. Here the laid sheets are pressed mechanically for a more consistent weight.

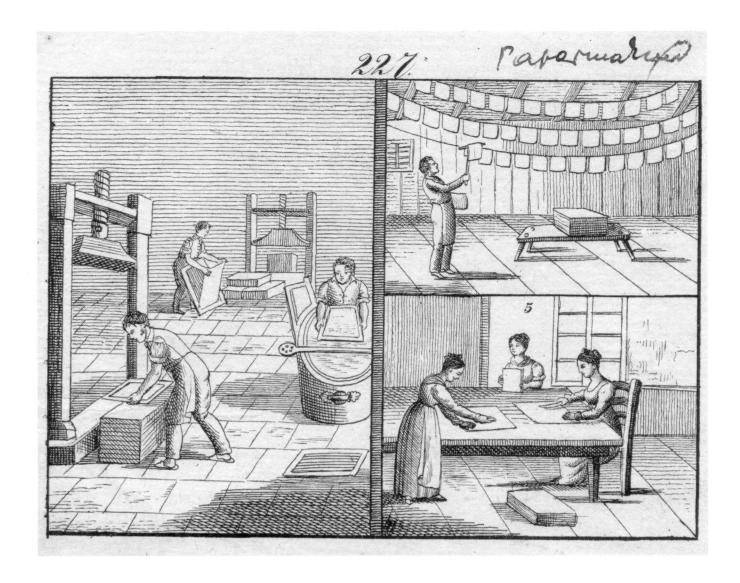

made its way to the Middle East and mills were built in Cairo, Baghdad and Morocco. The Arabs redeveloped the Chinese process slightly, mainly because they lacked some of the raw materials of the original recipe, so they compensated by making the paper entirely from rags and then coating it with starch paste. Necessity is the mother of invention, as they say, and the result of the Arab experiments was a fine-looking paper with a good surface for writing. Such was the desirability of this new substance that mills then spread to Spain and Sicily.

Japanese washi

Meanwhile the Japanese had been importing Chinese paper since around AD 300 and it had become an important commodity. In AD 610 a Korean Buddhist monk called Doncho was sent to Japan. He was an outstanding scholar who knew how to make paints and paper and it is thought that under his guidance the Japanese developed their own small-scale paper-making process. However, the Japanese found the Chinese style of paper too fragile so they set about creating their own version using plant fibres such as hemp and mulberry leaves. Their paper, called 'washi', was more durable than the Chinese version and less prone to insect damage.

Washi was soon widely used by the government, by nobles and also by the monks who copied religious scripts. The demand pushed the Japanese paper-making industry to expand and develop quickly. Techniques for making washi were passed down from generation to generation, and new materials added. Eventually washi became an art form that encompassed cultural and religious beliefs, and was thought to reflect the soul and spirit of the maker. It is still available today, and commonly used in decorative papercrafting.

EDUCATION MATERNELLE.   SAZERAC   PHOT

Origami

It is thought that paper folding was brought to Japan by the same Buddhist monks that introduced paper in the 6th century, although some historians argue that this art must have developed in some form soon after the first appearance of paper.

In Japan, paper was used not just for the very important matter of record keeping but also to make screens and models that were incorporated into religious and secular ceremonies. Ceremonial folding is thought to have been practised in the simplest of forms as early as 1185, in certificate folding and the giving of gifts.

As paper-making developed in Japan, so did the art of paper folding, and this art was passed down through the generations. Nevertheless, it wasn't until 1797 that the first written instructions appeared, while the word 'origami'

Above: Photograph by Sazerac on a postcard ca. 1903. A mother watches as her son and daughter make origami figures.
Left: Kes Guebrelibanos, a priest, makes parchment books out of goat skin at the Debre Damo Monastery in Ethiopia, 1998.

wasn't used until the 1880s. Prior to this, paper folding was known by a variety of names including 'orikata', meaning folded shapes. Although paper folding was also developed in Spain and other parts of Europe during the 12th century, and in Arabia prior to that, it is widely understood that the Japanese are the inventors of the particularly complex and fine art form of paper folding known as origami.

Parchment and vellum

Europe was rather behind the times at this stage and paper didn't reach the region until after it had been developed in Arabia and the Middle East. Instead, those who could afford it and who had the skills to use it worked on parchment or vellum. Parchment originated in Pergamun, Asia Minor around the second century BC. Traditionally it was made from an animal skin, usually a sheep, by soaking the skin in lime, removing the hair, rubbing it and stretching it out to dry. Vellum is a form of parchment, usually made from calfskin and sometimes regarded as a more refined version of parchment. Both are still available today and are used mainly by calligraphers.

Many European manuscripts written by monks were made on parchment or vellum. This type of vellum should not be confused with the very fine, translucent paper available from paper stockists today which resembles tracing paper.

European paper

The type of paper manufactured in Europe came from the Arab tradition. During the 13th century the Italians improved upon the Arabian method of papermaking not by changing the materials but by introducing new manufacturing techniques. They adopted power from watermills, as was being used by the textile and milling industries of the time, and they introduced wire moulds and paper presses, which resulted in more even and consistent paper thicknesses and sheet sizes.

During the Middle Ages paper became more and more important as its potential was recognized, but it was still a very secretive business. Inevitably, though, the art spread and during the 15th and 16th centuries paper mills appeared throughout Europe.

Laid paper

From the 16th century until the 1750s nearly all paper was known as laid paper. This was made by dipping a mould into a vat of pulp, usually made from rotted rags diluted in water. The mould was made by laying a mesh of strong wire over a frame called a deckle, with the wires about 2.5 cm apart. On top of this finer wires were laid, this time closer together. After dipping the mould in the vat the water would be drained off and the wet sheet of paper placed on a piece of felt to dry before being treated. Every mould had its own watermark (see opposite). If you hold a piece of laid paper up to the light you'll see the grid pattern made by the wires of the frame, and this can be used today by historians to help check the authenticity of a print or other document of the past.

Wove paper

In around 1755 a man called James Whatman the Elder converted a paper mill in Kent, England, to make wove paper. He developed a new process that used a very fine woven wire in the mould to produce a much smoother and more uniform paper than ever before. This fine paper is said to have played an important role in the development of English watercolour because its smooth surface meant that there were no furrows for the paint to puddle in. In addition, this paper was treated in a gelatin bath of hooves and bones, which made the paper stronger than ever. And it had another advantage – it was less absorbent, which meant that paint could be moved over the surface and multiple layers of paint applied and then wiped off or scraped away without damaging the paper. Thomas Gainsborough, J M W Turner and John Sell Cotman are just three of the many artists who used Whatman's wove paper for their watercolours.

Industrialization

In 1799 a French engineer named Nicolas-Louis Robert invented the first machine to make paper continuously, but it wasn't until the 19th century that paper became fully industrialized. One reason for this was that between 1840 and 1880 ground wood pulp and chemical pulp mills were developed to produce rag substitutes. The wood pulp gave paper a fine, even texture and aided its ability to accept printing ink. Machines became larger and all the sequences in the paper-making process were now mechanized rather than performed by hand.

Modern paper

Changes in paper-making continued to occur into the 20th and 21st centuries when new chemicals and processes were introduced. Whereas once paper was so expensive and hard to find that only the privileged could procure it, nowadays it is readily available and inexpensive. There are also many more different types, each geared towards a particular purpose, such as folding, writing, painting, packaging, absorbing spills and so on. Indeed, it is used in so many aspects of our daily lives that it is difficult to conceive of life without it (see pages 16–20).

Most of our paper these days is made from by-products of the lumber industries, from waste such as wood chippings or thin, tree-top branches, to recycled paper and cardboard, which would otherwise be burned or thrown away. Much of it is made in huge industrial plants, but traditional methods of paper-making are still practised. With the renewed interest in these papers sparked by a growing papercraft industry, more and more delightful handmade and traditionally made papers are

Above: An umbrella maker in Bor Sang, known as the 'umbrella village', in Thailand. The umbrellas are made from a bamboo frame covered with brightly coloured mulberry paper.

coming on to the market. You can also buy specialist papers from around the world – in Asia exquisite handmade papers can be found that incorporate mulberry and banana fibres, for example. There are a number of simple paper-making kits available today, so you can even have a go at making it yourself using traditional methods, which is a satisfying addition to your papercraft skills.

Watermarks

Watermarks are designs or patterns that are added to paper during the paper-making process. A design is added to the mould that creates an impression so that the paper is thinner where the words, letters or designs are placed, and when the sheet is held up to the light, the design become more visible. The watermark usually denotes the manufacturer, although papers can be specially made so that the watermark contains a company logo or individual's initials.

THE USE OF PAPER

Paper has been put to many uses over the years and will no doubt continue to play a major role in our lives. We spend it and read it, make beautiful things with it, use it for protective clothing, decoration, padding and even to keep warm. It's one of modern life's essentials.

Paper is used for so many products these days that it would be impossible to list them all here. In fact, because of its use in packaging and communication, there's probably not a single industry that doesn't use paper every day. Here are just some of the developments to the paper industry in the last few hundred years.

Packaging

From very early times we have needed materials to hold, store and transport items, and now that paper and card is so readily available and inexpensive it has become the obvious material to fulfil these needs. Since it can be recycled it is also one of the most desirable options.

Paper bags or sacks have been around since about 1800 and the first commercial paper bags were used in Bristol, England in 1844. At first the bags were made from flat paper but in the late 19th century, Hermann Holscher invented the flat-paper-sack machine, which folded and stitched the paper to make sacks in one process. Margaret Knight (1838–1914), invented the first machine that could cut, fold and glue paper to make paper bags. Although her idea was at first dismissed, she went on to receive 26 patents for her devices.

When we think of packaging one of the first things to spring to mind are all those cardboard boxes. The Chinese invented cardboard in around 1600, but it wasn't until 200 years later that the first cardboard box was produced. Corrugated paper didn't appear until about 1856 when it was patented by two Englishmen, Healey and Allen, and at that time it was used to line hats. In 1871 Albert Jones, an American, patented a stronger corrugated cardboard for shipping glass bottles, and in 1870 another American, Robert Gair, invented the cardboard box. Twenty years later he went on to invent the corrugated cardboard box, which eventually replaced the wooden crate for shipping and for the general transportation of goods. The invention

of the breakfast cereal by W.K. Kellogg advanced paper packaging further because the cereal was supplied in a cardboard box.

Paper plates and cups

Disposable items for eating on the run are everywhere these days, but it wasn't the burger box that was first on the scene. Instead it was the paper plate, which was first used in 1904. This was followed by the paper cup, which was invented in 1908 so that a cup could be provided by a vending machine connected to a water cooler – a penny for a cup of cool water. The paper cups were called 'health cups' because they were single use, disposable items, and therefore helped to reduce the spread of germs. Later the inventor renamed them Dixie cups. Eventually, in 1946, the resulting company would collaborate with Coca Cola.

Wallpaper

The Chinese first used rice paper to line the walls of their homes as early as 200 BC but this type of paper was a long way from wallpaper as we know it. It was the British who first used wallpaper as a wall covering, although it was a Frenchman named Christophe-Philippe Oberkampf who invented the first machine for printing it in 1775, around the same time as the first machine to make continuous rolls of paper was invented by Nicholas Louis Robert. The first wallpapers were decorated with handmade drawings and often depicted nature. In the late 1700s these designs became very fashionable in both France and Britain.

Paper money

China invented the first coins in about 700 BC, and the first paper bank note in around AD 806. However, as production soared, so did inflation, so in 1455 the country decided to rely on coins instead. It would be a few hundred

years until paper money was widely used in Europe, while the US didn't use its own paper money until 1862.

Papier mâché

Papier mâché is French for 'chewed paper', which is a very apt description. It usually consists of paper strips or pulp, combined with a binding ingredient usually in the form of glue and water. Despite its name, papier mâché actually originates from China, as you might by now have come to expect, and examples have been found in China dating back to between 200 BC and AD 200. The Chinese used paper toughened by layers of lacquer to make many objects ranging from helmets to pots and furniture. Papier mâché then spread to Japan and eventually on to Europe.

Above: 19th-century Austrian sheet of mottoes and illustrations for children to cut out and put in their scrapbooks.

France and England, for example, first started producing papier mâché items during the 1670s and an interest in the craft continued to increase until it was widely practised during the 1800s, reaching its peak in 1860.

Although not as universally popular as in its heyday, papier mâché is still used today, both for leisure craft activities and for theatre props and staging, where its light weight is most useful. It also retains a place in folk crafts and is particularly popular in Spain and Mexico.

Papier mâché dolls were common during the 19th century, although references date back to around 1500. Sometimes only the head was made of papier mâché while the body was in cloth or leather. However, this type of doll lost popularity with the production of ceramic dolls' faces, which were easier to clean and more realistic.

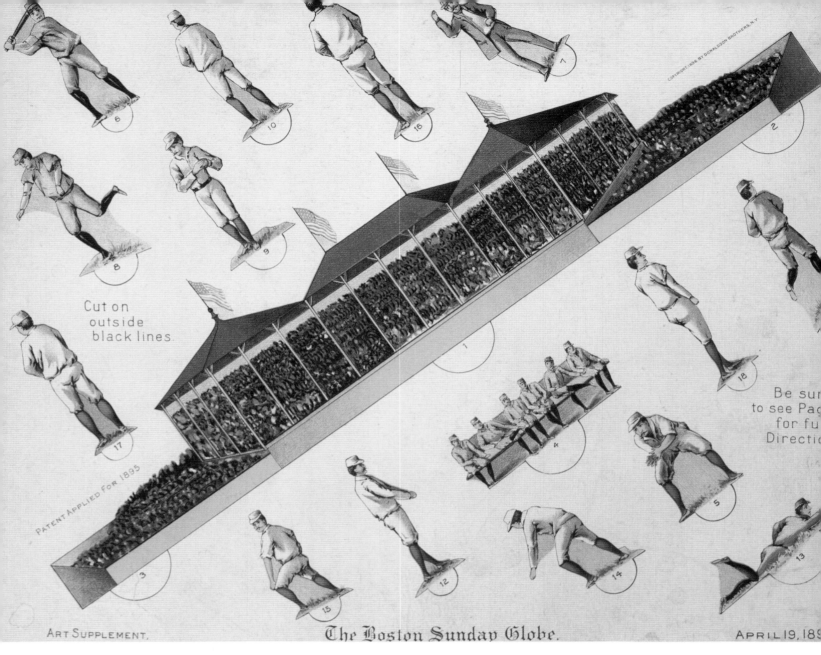

Cut on
outside
black lines.

PATENT APPLIED FOR 1895

COPYRIGHT 1896 BY DONALDSON BROTHERS N.Y.

Be sur
to see Pag
for fu
Directi

ART SUPPLEMENT,

The Boston Sunday Globe.

APRIL 19, 189

Paper dolls

Paper dolls have existed as long as the creation of paper itself, and they have been included in many religious and ceremonial rituals for centuries. Mostly these paper dolls are two-dimensional figures cut from paper on which paper clothes are laid. These dolls included both human and animal forms. In Japan around AD 900, paper figures were used in purification ceremonies. Folded paper figures were placed in little boats and put to sea, although these folded figures were three dimensional.

During the 1700s a stronger version of the paper doll became popular at the French Royal Court. These 'pantines' were made from painted cardboard with separate limbs that were joined together with thread so that the figures could be moved about. Later they became

Above: Cut-out paper baseball set from the *Boston Sunday Globe* ca. 1896. Readers are instructed to cut out the figures outside the black lines. These type of paper dolls were popular with both boys and girls.

quite popular children's toys. But they were nothing new: shadow puppets made from paper or card have been around for centuries, and you can probably guess where it's thought that they originally came from – China. Three-dimensional paper dolls have also got a long tradition. The first manufactured paper doll, 'Little Fanny', was made in 1810, and in 1859 the first printed doll to cut out and dress that we know of was published. It was in black and white and came with a set of clothes for children to paint and then fit on the doll. The 1900s saw

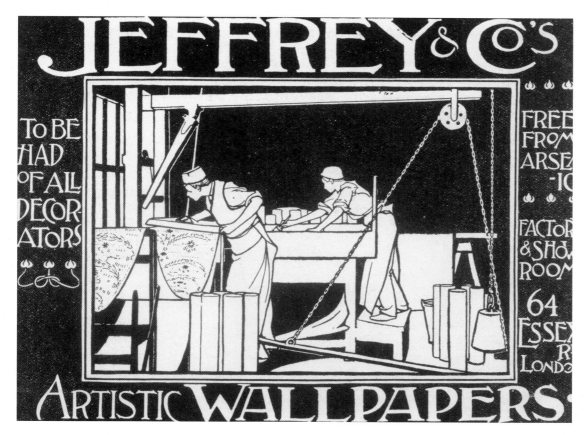

Above: Late 19th-century English wallpaper advertisement. Rolls of wallpaper are exquisitely hand painted and hung to dry.

an increase in trends for paper dolls and more magazines followed suit. It wasn't long before paper dolls were used in advertising, and often came as die-cut cards to keep. Children used them to paste into their scrapbooks. The 1930s to 1950s became known as the 'golden age of paper dolls' and celebrities and movie stars were reproduced as paper dolls. But their popularity nose-dived during the 1960s when plastic dolls such as Barbie were introduced.

Paper clothes

Paper has had many, many other uses in the past, but one of the most outlandish was the manufacture of paper clothes. These were introduced in the 1960s at the start of the throw-away society, along with paper plates and paper furniture. Some of these inventions were probably publicity stunts, such as the bikini that dissolved in water, which was designed in France. Perhaps not surprisingly, paper clothes never really caught on. They were uncomfortable to wear, got creased and had to be worn with care to avoid paper cuts. People were also afraid that the clothes would catch fire. In the end not many outfits were actually sold, but it wasn't all bad for the designers. For example, the Scott Paper Company made a

psychedelic Paisley shift dress for $1.25 and reportedly sold it for half a million US dollars.

Papercrafts

The popularity of papercraft has increased as paper has become cheaper and more readily available along with papercrafting tools such as glues, inks, paints, cutters and so on. Today, paper is used in many recreational activities including painting, drawing, calligraphy, card-making and scrapbooking. Specialist papers for such activities are on the increase and many local craft stores stock a wide range, but because of the Internet you can now also buy papers from around the world and find lovely exotic handmade papers for your crafting projects no matter where you live.

It seems that papercrafting fulfils our creative urges without necessarily requiring any great skill or any expensive tools and materials. There is much pleasure to be gained from the simplest — yet loveliest — of crafts.

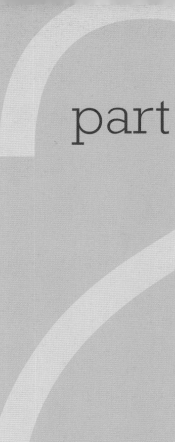

part

MATERIALS
AND
EQUIPMENT

PAPER TYPES

Paper is available in a vast array of colours, thicknesses and textures, so selecting the best type of paper for your project is a vital part of its design.

Paper classification

Paper is divided into three basic weights: lightweight paper, which includes tissue paper and vellum; medium-weight, which includes general craft and scrapbook paper; and heavyweight, such as embossed handmade paper and card or cardboard. When buying paper and card the abbreviation 'mic' indicates the thickness in microns, and 'gsm' refers to the weight in grams per square metre.

Another important classification is the paper's finish. Paper is available in a vast range of textures, colours and finishes, from plain to holographic metallic paper.

Grain

Paper and card have a grain, just as fabric does. The neatest folds and tears are made when they lie in the direction of the grain. To find the grain, gently bend the card or paper widthways and then lengthways without folding or creasing (see page 57). Whichever bends more easily is the direction of the grain.

Score your card or paper with a blunt knife or embossing tool before folding (see page 58). This will help prevent small creases forming and will give a neater fold when cardmaking.

Selecting card and paper

When selecting card and paper for any craft project first consider the theme. Colour, texture and weight are all vital to the success of the project and equally affect the result.

Plain white card is ideal for use as a base card in cardmaking and rubber stamping. The texture of the card could be smooth, or it can have an embossed texture such as hammer, linen or leatherette. These textures add a little extra impact even though they are subtle. Sumptuous card such as glitter and metallic card are best used in smaller quantities and need less embellishment to produce a stunning effect, while plainer card usually needs a few little extras, such as an ornate button or charm. When painting or using calligraphy, it is best to use paper specifically designed for this purpose, and to experiment until you obtain the desired result.

Decorative craft papers

These include stardust papers, felt paper, and holographic, shimmer, metallic and pearlescent effect paper and card. They are available from good craft shops and stationers, and a little usually goes a long way. Sometimes a tiny piece is all that is needed to transform a simple project. Often you'll find that these types of papers have an adhesive backing to make them even easier to use.

Two-tone card and paper have a different finish on each side, usually two toning colours or patterns. Other papers have a different core colour which is only visible once the paper or card is cut. A bevelled-edge cut (one made with a blade held at 45 degrees) will emphasize this, as will tearing to reveal a chamfered edge (see page 41).

Handmade paper

Many handmade papers contain dried leaves and petals as well as rag or recycled paper and they are more porous and thicker than standard machine-pressed card or paper. Tearing the edges of handmade paper will give an elegant and natural look. There isn't always a discernible grain as with machine-made paper.

Mulberry paper and banana paper include botanical ingredients. Mulberry paper can be given a lovely feathered edge when the paper is first wetted at the position of the required edge using a paintbrush and then the excess paper gently pulled away (see page 42).

Vellum

Traditional vellum was made from calfskin, which was exposed to lime, scraped and then stretched out to dry (see page 13), but today the name is given to good quality translucent paper, rather like tracing paper, that often has a subtle design of words or images. This modern vellum produces a lovely effect when embossed (the embossed areas turn white). It is non-porous so ink or paint will be slow drying, but it can be decorated with felt-tip pens or crayons successfully, if desired.

mulberry paper

crêpe paper

tissue paper

lace paper

origami paper

wallpaper

Japanese printed paper

cardstock

paper string

thick textured paper

The translucency of vellum makes it difficult to stick in place because the glue will often show even when dry, and some wet glues may even buckle the paper. A better idea is to use a sticker machine or to attach the paper with brads or eyelets, which have the advantage of adding a further decorative element.

Watercolour paper

This paper is designed to be wetted without losing its shape and is 'sized' to prevent the paint from sinking in and drying too quickly. It's ideal for painting on. When using light to medium-weight watercolour paper always tape it to a board before using very wet washes to prevent crinkling. This is known as stretching. Heavier weights can be used without stretching. Watercolour paper comes in white and a few pastel tints and is available in three basic textures: HP (smooth), Not (medium) and Rough.

Tissue paper

Tissue paper is very flimsy and is often used in papercrafts backed with something more substantial. It is good a good way to produce a stained-glass window effect when applied to a card aperture or frame.

Napkins

Patterned paper napkins can be used for a number of crafts including iris folding, découpage and origami. Napkins are economical and their thickness can be reduced by peeling away some of the layers. However colours and patterns are limited.

Origami paper

Origami paper is square and comes in plain colours or a variety of delicate patterns. It is designed to crease easily and its light weight and fine grain help to ensure that it holds the crease. It can also be used for layering in Oriental-style projects. Most of these papers are either 15 or 7.5 cm square.

Wallpaper

This is a thick, usually inexpensive paper that can be used for collage, découpage, layering and general cardmaking. Save scraps of leftover wallpaper from home improvement projects or look out for end-of-line discount offers.

Heavy-weight paper and card

Heavyweight paper or card can be used as a base for cardmaking and is often referred to as cardstock. This comes in many colours and has a smooth texture. The ideal weight for cardmaking is 240 to 280 gsm. For added decoration this type of card can be given a corrugated finish. You can buy it already corrugated or use a small hand-held crimping machine to crimp most papers or lightweight card yourself (see page 34).

Scrapbook paper

Usually 30 cm square, scrapbooking paper is designed to suit the popular needs of scrapbook enthusiasts. The paper is usually acid and lignin free so that it will not damage photographs even over a long period of time, unlike ordinary papers. Scrapbook paper varies in thickness and some types are double-sided with different patterns and colours on the reverse. Scrapbook paper has a white core when exposed, so can be used to produce a chamfered edge effect (see page 41).

Blank greetings cards

Cardmaking has become a popular leisure activity and to make life easier for the crafter, paper manufacturers now produce a range of blank cards. You can buy these in a large range of plain colours, different finishes and patterns. They are now available in several different shapes with single or double folds, some with apertures.

Envelopes

Readymade envelopes can be purchased for cardmaking. They are usually available in standard sizes to match the blank greetings cards and come in an increasing range of colours. You can also find them in unusual finishes to match specific cards, and some are specially designed to suit seasonal celebrations such as Christmas and Easter or have special birthday or wedding motifs.

card blanks

découpage sheet

vellum

gift tags

corrugated cardboard

newspaper

shredded printer paper

scrapbook paper

quilling tool

sticky-backed plastic

quilling paper

gift box

GLUES AND ADHESIVES

Adhesives are available to suit different needs and purposes. Always read the label to ensure that the product is suitable. The general types of adhesive are wet adhesives such as glue, and dry adhesives such as sticky tape.

Wet adhesive

Stick glue is a paper glue on a handy stick. It is easy to use and ideal for sticking lightweight pieces of paper together. It is not suitable for scrapbooking.

Multi-purpose glue is ideal for sticking different types of materials together, such as gluing sequins onto paper or for adding metallic charms to cards.

PVA (polyvinyl acetate) glue is a white water-based glue that dries clear. It is often used to secure pressed flowers to card and paper, for découpage images and for collage projects. It can be diluted with water to make a clear varnish.

Glue pens look like felt-tip pens but release glue instead of colour. They come in acid-free versions which are suitable for scrapbooking.

Instant-bonding adhesive creates a strong, almost instant bond between a variety of materials but it is not ideal for sticking paper to paper because paper is so porous. Silicone adhesive is a strong multi-purpose glue often used in découpage to coat the motifs.

Hot glue sticks are used for adding heavy items such as buttons and charms to your projects and are a good alternative to instant-bonding adhesive. The glue is applied with a glue gun that heats and melts the glue ready for use. The glue dries and hardens as it cools. It takes a little practice to use a glue gun effectively, but once mastered most users become firm fans. This glue is not suitable for children.

Aerosol adhesives are great for sticking paper or photographs to paper but it can be difficult to control the amount of adhesive applied. To protect the work area, place the paper item upside down in an old shoe box before spraying. Both repositionable and permanent varieties are available. Use only in well-ventilated areas.

Glitter glue comprises clear glue with pieces of glitter mixed into it. It comes in a range of sparkling colours and in easy-to-use tubes. It tends to be slow drying and is usually applied as the final embellishment.

Dry adhesive

Adhesive spots are available on a roll. You can buy non-permanent, and permanent varieties as well as acid-free versions which are designed with the scrapbooker in mind. Press the item onto the adhesive spot and then peel it away from the backing roll. The item can then be stuck in place. Adhesive spots eliminate mess and drying time, and are easy to use. They are available in a number of sizes.

Double-sided tape is often used to stick mats or mounts together when layering paper and card. It is especially well suited for cardmaking because it is quick and easy to use. It comes in several thicknesses and sheets of double-sided tape are now available to cover larger areas. Glitter, sand or accent beads can be shaken onto the sheets to create sparkly self-adhesive paper. The clear sticky tape used for packaging is not suitable for most papercrafts because it will always show on the finished project and deteriorates quickly.

Roller adhesive is another type of dry adhesive. It comes in a dispenser or roller and is usually permanent. It is rolled onto the paper to release the adhesive. It can be used with tissue paper as it is not bulky.

Foam pads give a raised, three-dimensional effect to a project and are often used in découpage; they can also be used to give die cuts a raised finish. They are sticky on both sides, but require no drying time. These pads are often difficult to remove if a mistake is made.

Sticker machines are available in different sizes and can be used with repositional or permanent adhesive cartridges. Some machines can also laminate or add magnetic backings for making fridge magnets and so on. They are ideal for sticking small punched shapes in place. To reduce waste, position items together in the tray. These machines cut out much of the mess associated with glue and also eliminate drying time. Very thin paper can be strengthened by running it through a sticker machine and then placing it on thicker backing card or paper.

dry adhesive strip

stick glue

all-purpose glue stick

6-mm double-sided tape

instant-bonding glue

glue pen

PVA glue

clear all-purpose glue

adhesive line

super-strength glue

spray adhesive

tiny adhesive spots

silicone adhesive

INSTANT GRRRiP
WHITE CRAFT CEMENT
TACKY ON CONTACT
DRIES CLEAR
Contents 4 Fl. Ozs. (113.4 Grams)

SPRAY ADHESIVE
PERMANENT

UHU
The All Purpose Adhesive

clear silicone adhesive
decoupage, tolling,
stained glass, mosaic
use on metal, glass, ceramic,

FASTENERS AND EMBELLISHMENTS

Three-dimensional objects such as beads, brads and charms can be used instead of glue to fasten pieces of paper or card together and add an extra special quality to any project.

Brads

Brads are winged fasteners that are available in round, square and novelty shapes, and in a vast range of colours. To use a brad, a hole must be made in the paper first, either with a needle, small punch or piercing tool. Now the brad can be inserted into the hole and the wings opened out on the reverse to secure it. Brads are a good way to secure paper such as vellum as glue would be visible from the front. Brads can be used to secure more than one sheet at a time, and are a great way to make mini-books for scrapbooking. They are usually inexpensive embellishments and require no special tools.

Eyelets

Eyelets are small ring-shaped embellishments. A small hole is made in the paper into which the ring sits. They can be purely decorative or used to fasten pieces of paper together in place of adhesives. They can also be laced together for added decoration.

To attach an eyelet you will need a special eyelet setter and should ideally work on a protective mat, called a setting mat. There are different types of setters available, but they work on the same principle. The traditional eyelet setter looks a bit like a bradawl or screwdriver and is used in conjunction with a small hammer. One end of the tool has a small punch to make a hole and the other end sets the eyelet once it is placed in the hole. Spring loaded eyelet tools are also available; this eliminates the use of a hammer. The method you decide to use is a matter of personal choice.

Eyelets come in a range of sizes and so different sized tools are available, but if you think you might want to use eyelets frequently you could invest in a kit, which comes with setters of different sizes.

Buttons and charms

Buttons come in many different sizes, styles and colours, from the type that you use on clothing to more elaborate novelty ones made from porcelain and glass. All can be glued in place or secured with a few simple stitches.

Charms are used in much the same way as buttons and usually contain a loop for attachment. Buttons and charms can be used in the same way as brads to secure mini envelopes, tags and pockets, for example, or as a fastening on a gateway-fold card or scrapbooking page.

Sequins and beads

Beads and sequins are available in different sizes, shapes, colours and finishes. You can glue them in place with a strong glue or use a thread. Take a single stitch up through the paper, through the sequin or bead and back through the paper beside the sequin. Alternatively, sequins can be attached with a small bead at the centre. Bring the needle up through the paper, through the sequin and then through the small bead. Now take the thread back through the same holes in the sequin and paper. This creates a very neat and attractive finish. You can attach beads and sequins at random or use several to create three-dimensional borders or pretty trails.

Other types of fasteners

These include safety pins, coloured staples, and stitched ribbons and threads. All of these can be used to join paper items together and will provide a durable finish. Try attaching small tags decorated with ribbon to a card using mini pegs, or hang a number of cut-out shapes from a clothes line. Ribbon and string can also be threaded through punched holes or eyelets to create attractive patterns – an easy way to make a mini-book or closure.

buttons

tiny safety pins

pom-poms

adhesive gems

sewing thread

paperclips

flower spray

mini clothes pegs

embroidery thread

card embellishments

bead embellishments

pressed flowers

feathers

ribbon

CUTTING EQUIPMENT

There are a number of cutting tools on the market at the moment, each designed for a specific purpose or craft. Sometimes inexpensive general equipment is all that is needed. Many items can be used for the same purpose so it is really down to personal preference when choosing.

Craft knife

A craft knife is an essential tool used in most papercraft projects and it is also relatively inexpensive. Use it with a metal ruler and cutting mat to cut straight lines such as edges and apertures or to cut fine details.

Sharp scalpel blades are ideal for making precision cuts, and when the blade becomes blunt it can be replaced quite easily. Blades are available in different sizes and shapes to suit a variety of craft needs.

Disposable craft knives are also available. The blade and handle is usually one moulded piece so that the blade cannot be changed when it blunts. As with all sharp objects, dispose of it carefully.

Self-healing cutting mats are the perfect surface for cutting on. They not only protect the surrounding surface but make it easier to cut neatly and accurately. Most have a grid to help with measurements – useful for cutting apertures.

Craft scissors

General-purpose craft scissors will suit most tasks, but they must be kept sharp – keep a separate pair for cutting fabric, as paper scissors tend to blunt more easily. As with all tools, it is best to try before you buy. Choose a medium-sized pair with comfortable handles that will cut both paper and card. When using scissors, the preferred method is to make one cut using the full length of the blade while feeding the paper through the scissor blades.

There are a number of sizes and types of scissors available including pairs designed for left-handers or people without a strong grip. Découpage scissors are small with straight or curved blades for cutting intricate shapes. Tweezer scissors have very short blades and sprung arms, and can have curved blades. They are very good for cutting around small, complex shapes because they take small snips. These should only be used for cutting paper – it is usually easier to roughly cut around the motif with a large pair of scissors first.

Decorative edging shears

With shaped blades, these can be used to cut wavy, deckle, pinked or scalloped edges and more. They are a great way of adding subtle decoration to paper projects, mats and mounts. When making multiple cuts, line the scissors up with the last cut to obtain a neat, continuous pattern along the edge. Make a complete cut along the blade before repositioning the scissors.

Rotary cutters

These are basically round razor blades in a holder that are used in conjunction with a cutting mat and steel ruler. The handle is similar to that of a craft knife and the cut is achieved by rolling the wheel along the paper in line with the edge of the ruler. The cut can be changed from straight to deckle or even a perforated finish by changing the wheel. Rotary cutters are especially useful for cutting long, straight edges and can cut through two or more layers of paper at once. Always use with a cutting mat.

Guillotines and trimmers

It is much easier to achieve a straight edge with a guillotine or trimmer than with a pair of scissors or a craft knife so a more professional look is achieved. Both have gradation measurements marked on them to help with positioning.

Trimmers are available in a number of sizes and to suit a range of budgets. Some have interchangeable decorative blades, enabling you to cut wavy or perforated lines. The paper should be placed in the trimmer with the cut edge under the trimmer's ruler. Slide the handle, which secures the blade, along the ruler to make each cut.

Guillotines have a handle that is brought downward to chop the paper. Because the blade is more exposed these are not recommended for use with children, but they have the advantage that they will usually cut through thicker paper than a trimmer and can cut through several layers at once.

Decorative punches

Decorative punches are a fun and easy way to cut paper shapes. They are available in many different sizes and designs, and each one produces two decorative shapes – the punched paper motif and the hole left behind.

With a little care it is relatively easy to line up a punch with patterns or shapes on the paper being cut. Turn the punch over and you will be able to see the hole being cut and position the paper accordingly. Place the upside down punch on a flat surface before pressing down and punching the shape. Punches are usually more suitable for lightweight paper rather than card, but a punch aid will enable thicker card to be used.

Plier punches

These are used for putting holes or small shapes into card. They can be used to punch a hole in the top of a gift tag so that ribbon can be threaded through, for example.

Edge cutters

Border punches have repeat patterns that can be used to cut decorative borders. They are usually more ornate than the borders you can cut with decorative shears. Care is needed to line up the punch for a continuous border.

Corner punches are used to create decorative corners on rectangles or squares of paper. Designs range from simple rounded corners to more intricate designs and are usually very effective. The sides of the punch keep the paper in place, making it easy to achieve professional results.

Frame punches

This type of punch removes an area of background surrounding a shape or motif (rather than punching out the motif itself), creating an elegant silhouette. The cut shape can be saved and used so there is no waste.

Sharpening punches

If a punch becomes blunt, don't throw it away. Instead punch some shapes out of aluminium foil or waxed paper, which will sharpen it up.

Oval and circle cutters

There are different types of oval and circle cutters on the market. Some have an adjustable arm and cut between 2.5-cm and 20-cm circles; others resemble a compass. They contain a tiny blade that cuts the shape as it is rotated. The shape can be cut out of card or paper to leave a negative space or used in the same way a punched shape.

Centre punches

Most punches must be used quite close to the paper's edge. If you want to make a cut further in you have several options.

Long-reach punches have long handles to reach further over the paper. They are useful for cutting apertures in single-fold cards, or negative confetti-style shapes randomly over paper – be sure to save the cut-outs for use as embellishments in other projects.

Paddle punches can be placed anywhere on a page, making them highly versatile, but they tend to cut quite small shapes. These are basically shaped cutters on the end of a handle. You place the cutter where you want it over the card and hit it with a special hammer to make the cut. For best results use the cutter on a hard surface with a cutting mat underneath your paper to protect the work surface and prolong the life of the cutter. You can also use paddle punches to cut fabric and foil.

Shape cutters

Stencil systems work with stencils that have shallow cutting lines cut in them. They are available in various shapes such as stars, tags, envelopes and ovals, and make it easy to cut photo mounts. You will need a special stencil, cutting mat and a swivel-blade cutting knife (see page 31). As with all such tools, practice makes perfect.

Die-cutting machines are now available to the home crafter. You can buy a large range of cutting plates which tend to be more elaborate than punch designs and cut through a wider range of materials including fabric. The shapes can be layered to produce three-dimensional motifs and alphabets, and some machines will also emboss. However, they are designed for the keen papercrafter, and can be very expensive.

giant punch

paddle punches

decorative punch

edging shears

circle border punch

plier punches

patterned border punch

TEXTURING EQUIPMENT

Textured effects can be added to paper and card using a number of methods. Although often very simple, the results can transform a humble sheet of paper or card into something much more sophisticated.

Paper crimpers

Paper crimpers, or 'ribblers' as they are sometimes called, are simple devices that add a corrugated texture to paper. Paper is passed through rollers, which crimp it so that it becomes corrugated. Paper can be folded and passed through at different angles to achieve different effects. For example, a leaf shape folded in half and passed through at 45 degrees will produce a vein effect when unfolded.

Piercing tool

A piercing tool enables tiny holes to be made in paper and card. Templates are also available which allow intricate patterns to be made. The result is a textured, lacy pattern that is quite effective, especially when the paper is layered on top of metallic or dark paper as this will emphasize the pattern. A sharp embroidery needle could also be used with similar results.

Puff paints and pens

Some paints and felt-tips contain a substance that puffs up as the colour dries to create a three-dimensional effect. Used sparingly these can be very effective.

Embossing tool

A tool with either a stylus or a small metal ball at the end is used for embossing. It is used in conjunction with an embossing stencil to create raised or embossed areas and it can also be used to score a crease in cards when run along the edge of a metal ruler (see page 58).

Embossing stencils

Embossing stencils are used to create a raised or indented design on paper. It is easy to do. Simply place an embossing stencil under your paper then use a stylus or embossing tool to run along the lines of the stencil and transfer the design. Either place the paper over a light source such as a lightbox to help you with positioning or use two-part stencils which are positioned with one section over the paper and the other underneath it. If you wish the raised side of the stencil to be the right side, your image will be reversed. Remember to take this into account with letters by embossing a reverse image. Stencils are made of plastic or brass.

Heat embossing

Embossing powder can be used to create raised designs. Load a rubber stamp with a slow-drying ink or embossing ink and stamp your image then sprinkle embossing powder on to the wet ink and heat with a heat gun to melt the powder. Use a contrasting coloured powder for bold results or match the paper for subtle effects.

Coloured sand and glitter

Coloured sand and glitter are great for adding texture. Apply some glue, sprinkle on the sand or glitter and leave to dry. Now shake off the excess onto a large sheet of paper, so you can easily return the leftovers to the pot.

Beads

Small accent beads – tiny coloured balls – can be sprinkled onto glue like glitter, added to papier mâché paste, or even concealed under a thin layer of tissue paper for added texture. Beads with holes, such as tiny seed beads, may also be used in this way, or simply stitched on randomly to make a textured background.

Smooth embossing

Rub your embossing tool over a wax candle so that it will glide more easily over the paper and is less likely to tear it.

accent beads

embossing powders

3-colour ink pad

embossing stencils

felt-tip markers

coloured sand

puff-up writing pen

paper crimper

ink pad and wooden stamp

ADDING COLOUR

Colour can either make or break a design. Choose a colour that harmonizes with the overall theme and style of the project, using softer colours for feminine, baby and vintage projects, or primary colours for children's themes.

Unifying effects

An easy way to unify a design is to work in shades of the same colour or keep to just two or three different colours, such as blue and yellow. Choose similar colours for harmony, such as lilac, pink and blue or opposites like red and green for a bolder, brighter statement.

Watercolour paints

These are useful for creating tints and pale washes, and for colouring in stamped images. Ideally work on watercolour paper or handmade paper – lightweight papers are least suited for watercolour paints or washes.

Acrylic paints

This type of paint can be used straight from the bottle or tube, or thinned by adding water. It is opaque and very versatile. Once dry, it is water resistant.

Specialist craft paints

Dimensional paints usually come in squeezy bottles and the nozzle has an applicator tip. Droplets or beads are easily made and fun to apply – they make great borders.

Pearlescent and metallic craft paints can be bought ready mixed, or as powders to add to other mediums. Some have interference effects so that they look different depending on whether they are applied to light or dark coloured paper.

Leafing and gel pens

Leafing pens contain metallic inks such as copper, silver or gold leaf. The paint is applied much like a marker pen, and is easy to control. An easy way to add elegant highlights.

Gel pens have a similar use, but the ink has a shiny gel-like appearance. They are available in a wider range of shades and finishes from metallic to mat, neon and pastel.

Chalks

Chalks create a subtle yet rather lovely effect. They can be blended with cotton wool or a sponge-tipped applicator to remove hard lines. Apply chalk to a chamfered edge for a pretty effect (see page 41).

Coloured pencils and pastels

Coloured pencils are easy to control. Shading and blending are achieved by varying the pressure on the tip. Watercolour pencils are also available. These can be applied to wet or dry paper or, if desired, water can be applied with a brush to the pencil work afterwards, to soften it. A wet brush can also be used to blend different colours together. Pastels are available in pencil or stick form and can be used in the same way as chalks.

Ink

Liquid ink is mainly used in calligraphy, but it can also be used in the same way as watercolour paint. Ink pads may contain dye ink or pigment ink. Many are acid free for use in scrapbooks.

Dye ink is quick drying and can be applied to most coated paper. It can be used on vellum and is water resistant so that the images can be painted afterwards.

Pigment inks, on the other hand, are slow drying and are used for heat embossing (see page 34). They are only suitable for porous paper and will not dry fully on glossy paper.

Glitter

Very fine or ultra-fine coloured glitter can look exquisite. Glue can be applied with a fine-tipped applicator and the glitter sprinkled on top while it is still wet.

Glitter glue is simply glitter suspended in glue and is usually applied directly from the tube or bottle. It is great for adding highlights and very easy to use.

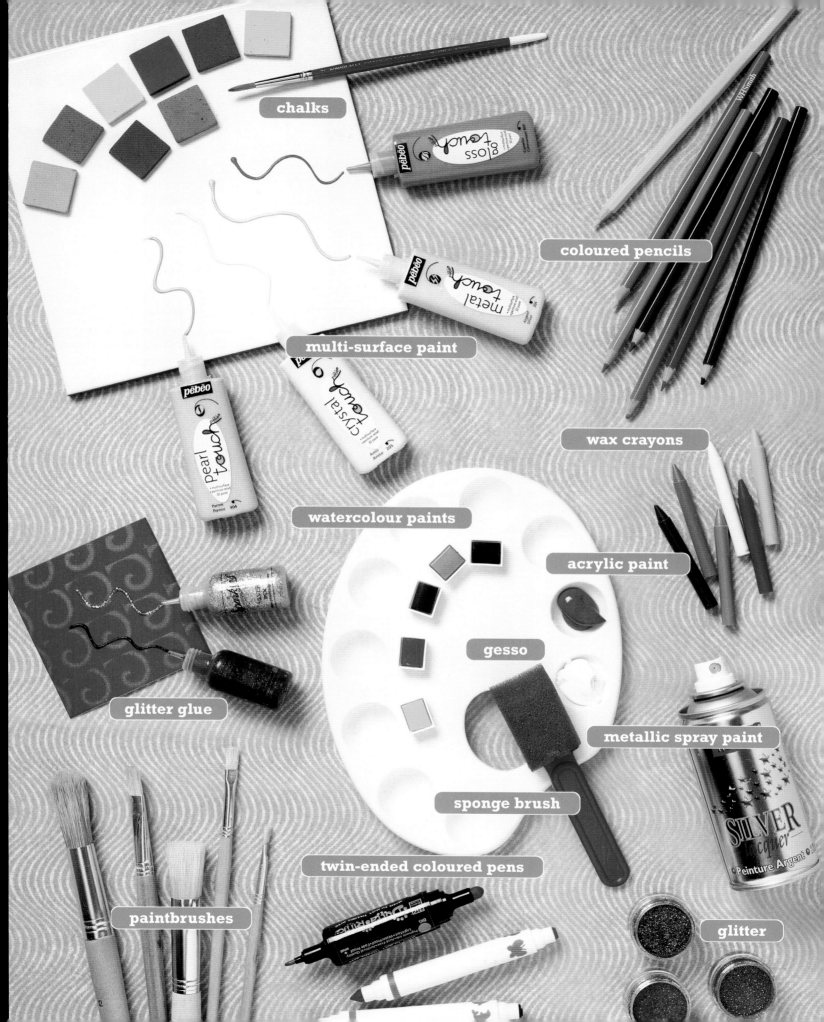

chalks

coloured pencils

multi-surface paint

wax crayons

watercolour paints

acrylic paint

gesso

glitter glue

metallic spray paint

sponge brush

twin-ended coloured pens

paintbrushes

glitter

part 3

TECHNIQUES AND PROJECTS

TEARING

Tearing paper produces a lovely soft-textured edge that is particularly effective where you want a softened look. The effect can be exaggerated or moderated depending on the technique and type of paper used. Experiment with a variety of manufactured and handmade papers until you have the right effect for your project.

Types of paper

Most paper can be torn instead of cut. Tearing works especially well with the vast range of handmade papers available today. Experiment with different tearing techniques using a range of papers including vellum, mulberry paper, tissue paper and scrapbooking papers to discover all the lovely effects you can create. Always practice on a scrap of your chosen paper to find out which technique works best for your current project.

Using a ruler

Tearing against a ruler produces a very straight but natural edge and you'll find that the technique gives you good control. Lay a metal ruler along the paper in the desired position and hold it with your left hand if you are right-handed. Use your right hand to tear the paper upwards, against the ruler, while maintaining a firm pressure on the ruler with your left hand, as shown. Reverse the instructions if you are left-handed.

Creating a chamfered edge

With some of the thicker types of handmade paper you'll find that when you tear paper upwards and away from your body, a chamfered edge appears where some of the white paper underneath is left behind. This effect can be quite pretty, and you can either leave the white of the paper as it is to provide a decorative contrast or apply chalks, ink or paint in toning colours to create a more subtle layering effect.

Avoiding a chamfered edge

A chamfered edge won't always be suitable for your project. If your paper always seems to tear with a chamfered edge and you don't want it to you have two options: you can either turn the paper over to tear it so that the chamfered edge is on the underside or you can tear against a ruler, as shown.

Feathered edge

This technique works particularly well on thin, fibrous handmade papers such as mulberry paper.

1 A feathered edge is more irregular than an edge torn against a ruler, but more controlled than tearing freestyle. Use a small artist's paintbrush to paint water along the paper where you want the feathered edge to be.

2 Gently pull the edge of the paper away along the damp line to leave a soft, feathered finish.

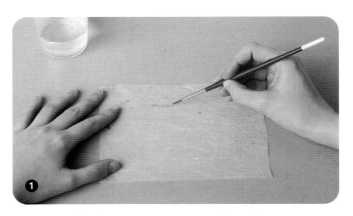

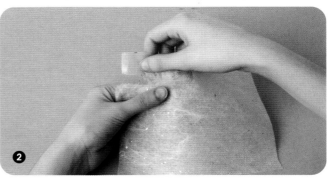

Background shapes

Use this technique to create feathered backing papers for cards. Try the following easy shapes:
- heart
- star
- circle
- flower

Templates

You can tear paper into specific shapes using wooden or acrylic blocks or special templates. For original or unique shapes, make your own templates from thick cardboard. Use the same technique as when tearing against a ruler (see page 41), pressing the block down on to the paper with one hand and tearing the paper upwards with the other. If you are using your own cardboard template, make a set of varying sizes for layered paper projects.

Attaching torn paper

Dry torn or feathered paper can be attached to paper or card with glue, double-sided tape or a sticker-making machine. If you are using vellum you'll find that glue can show through and look messy so either use special vellum glue or attach the paper with brads or eyelets. These also work well with most other paper types.

Aging effects

Torn paper can be crumpled and then coloured with diluted cold tea, walnut ink, or distressing inks to produce an aged effect for a heritage look. Chalks and metallic waxes can also be rubbed along the edges or the folds of the paper to enhance the effect.

Pockets

If you want to attach tags, cards, photos or other items to your projects like cards or scrapbook pages, why not use a pocket? It is quick and easy to make and provides an opportunity for further decoration. For a soft effect, tear the paper along the opening edge of the pocket or, if all the edges of the pocket will be on show, you can tear them all. Use double-sided tape along three sides of the pocket to attach it to the page.

Tearing tips

- Don't expect tearing to look good every time. Torn edges tend to work best on papers with natural fibres, especially handmade papers, and patterned papers with pretty or natural themes.
- Always test the effect on a scrap of your chosen paper first because some papers tear more neatly than others.
- Try tearing the paper both horizontally and vertically because it won't always look the same. The neatest tears are made when they lie in the direction of the paper grain.

Writing set

A note written on handmade paper is thoughtful and personal. Embellish it with torn paper, golden sequins and eyelets for an exquisite touch. Use the same paper to line a set of matching envelopes.

YOU WILL NEED:

- small ready-made envelope to use as a template
- handmade paper for each envelope and notelet
- decorative paper for each envelope and notelet
- gold sequins and other small embellishments of your choice, such as eyelets
- soft pencil
- ruler
- eraser
- paper glue

A 14 x 21 cm notelet (folded in half) will fit a standard 11.5 x 16 cm envelope.

1 Open out a ready-made envelope to create a template. Place it on your sheet of handmade paper and lightly draw around it using a soft pencil. Set the template aside and tear out your new envelope along the pencil lines, using a ruler to create straight edges (see page 41). Use an eraser to remove any remaining pencil lines.

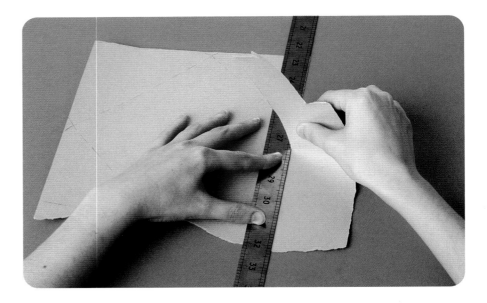

2 Following the instructions in step one, make a slightly smaller envelope liner from decorative paper, then use suitable paper glue to attach it to the envelope.

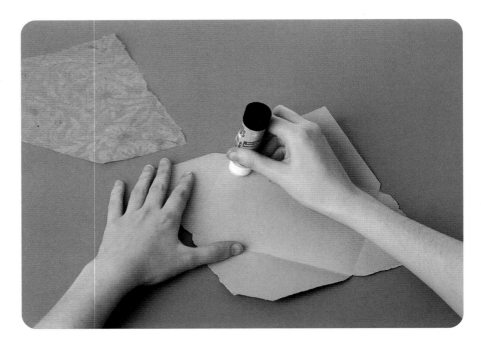

3 Fold the edges of the envelope inwards, using your template envelope as a guide to the positions of the folds. Glue the tip of the lower flap to the two side flaps, as shown, making sure that you don't get any glue inside the envelope or the whole thing will stick together.

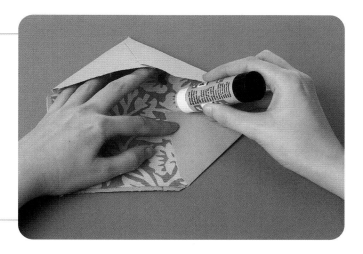

4 To make the notelet, use the ruler method (see page 41) to tear out a rectangle of paper that will fit inside your envelope. Tear strips of matching or coordinating decorative paper to make a chamfered edge and stick the strips along the edge of the notelet, as shown.

5 Finally, embellish the notelet with one or more torn heart shapes and gold sequins or eyelets, remembering to leave enough blank space on the notelet to write your message. (You will find it easiest to make your hearts if you tear them around a card template as explained on page 42.)

Gift tags and paper

Torn handmade paper decorated with corrugated cardstock, elegant copper wire and foil motifs make simple yet stylish gift tags. Complete the set by decorating your own gift wrap in coordinating colours.

YOU WILL NEED:

- handmade paper
- corrugated cardstock
- ready-made copper foil or copper wire embellishment for each tag
- raffia
- ruler
- hole punch
- instant-bonding adhesive
- all-purpose glue
- Plain coloured tissue papers for the gift wrap
- water spray
- iron
- bleach
- artist's brush
- acrylic paint
- toothbrush
- newspaper

1 Make a rectangle of handmade paper the size you want your tag, tearing it against the side of a ruler to produce a rough edge (see page 41). Punch a hole near the top. Cut a smaller rectangle of corrugated card, cutting along the grooves and at exact right angles. Stick the copper embellishment on the card with instant-bonding adhesive and stick the paper and card together with all-purpose glue. Use raffia to attach the tag.

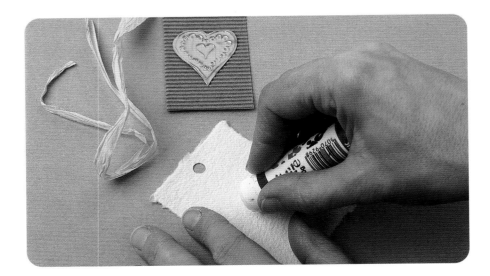

2 To decorate the gift wrap with swirls, spray coloured tissue paper lightly all over with water. Press the paper with a medium hot iron, lifting the iron to move it rather than dragging it across the paper. Lay the tissue paper on newspaper, then paint quick swirls over the surface with bleach using a fine artist's brush. Take care not to drip or splatter any of the bleach.

3 To create a speckled pattern, cover a large area with newspaper and lay a sheet of wrinkled tissue paper in the centre. Mix some acrylic paint to the consistency of light cream. Dip the bristles of the toothbrush in the paint and shake off the excess. Holding the brush clear of the edge of the paper, run your finger across the bristles to splatter tiny droplets of paint over the paper. Alternatively, use a cocktail stick instead of your finger to splatter the paint. Repeat as necessary.

Painting tip
Avoid moving the brush over the paper because it may drip. Instead, turn the paper as you need to so that your working area is in front of you. To give the pattern greater depth, use two or three toning paint colours.

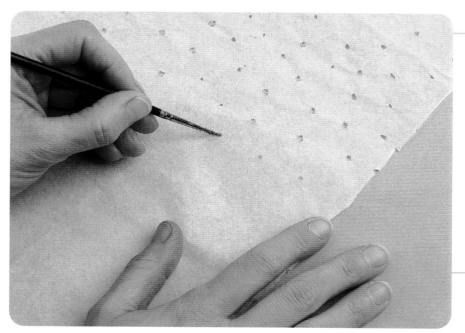

4 To create a polka-dot decoration, paint tiny spots over the entire surface of a plain piece of tissue paper with a fine artist's brush. Allow to dry completely. Spray the reverse side of the paper with water and press with an iron, taking care not to drag the iron across the paper or the paint could smudge.

Scented flower ball

Use scented papers to make a delightful flower ball to hang in a wardrobe or place on your pillow. Alternatively, spray handmade papers with alcohol-free perfume to achieve a similar effect.

YOU WILL NEED:

- 10-cm-diameter polystyrene ball (large ball) or 8-cm-diameter ball (small ball)
- 10-cm scrap of thick cardboard to make a flower template
- 8-cm squares of scented handmade paper
- 21 x 30 cm sheet of green tissue paper
- rocaille or seed beads
- flat round beads
- sequins
- dressmaker's pins
- 20 cm of 2-cm-wide organza ribbon for each ball
- all-purpose glue (optional)

To make a large ball you will need 90 paper squares (to make 30 flowers), 30 rocaille beads, flat beads, sequins, and pins (plus extra to attach paper and ribbon). The small ball requires 60 paper squares (to make 20 flowers) and 20 of the beads, sequins and pins.

1 Make a flower petal template from thick cardboard (see page 185). Place the template on the handmade paper and, pressing it down firmly with one hand, tear the paper up around it with the other hand, as shown. Make three sets of petals per flower.

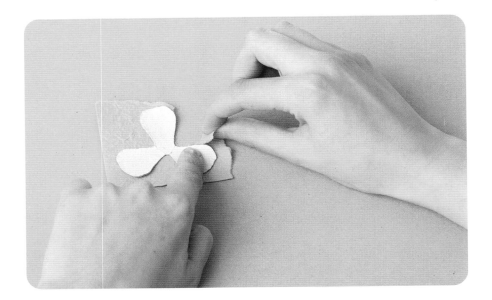

2 Gently shape the petals with your fingers, or use a shaping tool. Hold the petal shapes in the palm of your hand and rub the individual petals in a circular motion to create a natural concave shape.

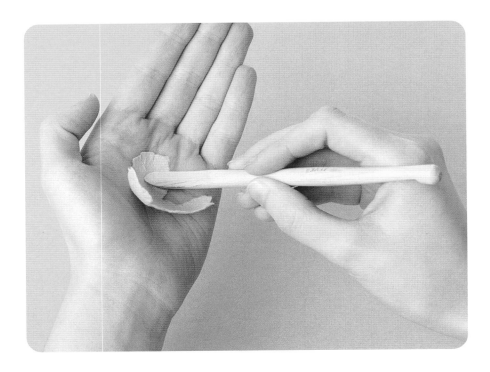

3 Cover the polystyrene ball with green tissue paper using either pins or all-purpose glue. Next, make a hanger from the ribbon by folding it in half and attaching the ends to the ball with pins or glue.

To assemble each flower, first arrange three petal sets together then place a 1 to 2 cm piece of torn green tissue paper in the centre. Take a pin and thread on a rocaille followed by a flat round bead and then a sequin, with the sequin facing towards the pinhead. Now pass the pin through the flower centre, securing all layers. Press the pin into the ball. Repeat, spacing the flowers evenly.

Cardmaking tip
Use the leftover scraps of handmade paper to make a card or gift tag. Even tiny scraps of paper can be used to create a decorative collage over a paper heart-shape, as shown here.

FOLDING

This amazing papercraft technique requires few tools except a bone folder and something to score with, yet it enables you to transform a two-dimensional sheet of paper or card into anything from a card to a complex origami model. Give texture to your designs with pleats or crimps or use folding to create items that can be both practical and beautiful.

Testing the grain

To test which way the grain runs, hold the paper by one edge and see how the paper bends. If it bends more one way than the other that is the way the fibres are going. This is the direction of the grain.

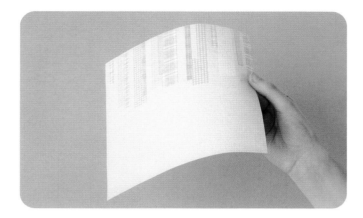

Folding large sheets of paper

To fold a big sheet of paper neatly you will need to work on a large flat surface. Fold the paper over and hold the top corners together with one hand. With the other hand smooth the paper gently but firmly towards the fold and flatten it out. Work your way down the paper still holding the edges together with one hand and flattening up to the fold with the other hand.

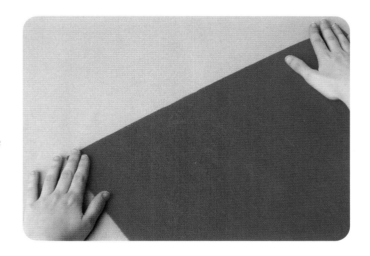

Folding origami paper

Origami paper is especially created to fold easily. It is lightweight and its fibres are randomly spread so that there is no grain. It will fold in any direction with ease. To crease origami paper, start in the middle of the fold-line on the paper. Press along the fold-line first in one direction and then return to the centre to crease the rest of the fold.

Scoring thick paper and card

Card and thick paper will need scoring before folding. This dents the fibres along the line so it is easier to fold and creates a guide for the fold to follow. Scoring needs to be accurate for successful folding. You can score a crease either by grazing the surface of the paper with a craft knife or by making a dent with a blunt object such as an embossing tool or metal knitting needle. If you are using a knife be careful to graze the surface rather than cutting clean through – if in doubt, use the unsharp edge of the knife to score with. Make sure you score with the grain.

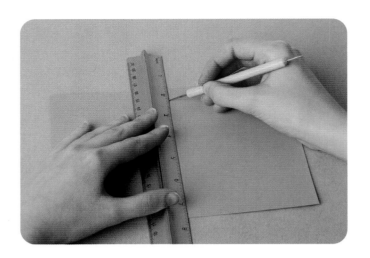

Folding handmade paper

Handmade papers, especially those with lumps and bumps such as mulberry paper, are not easy to fold. The bumps, which are often seeds or plant fibres, make the paper difficult to score as the ruler won't lay flat. It is easier to fold this type of handmade paper without scoring first. Use the same method as for folding large sheets of paper (see page 57).

Making a card blank

To make a card blank, first cut the card or cardstock to the appropriate size. If the card has a right side and a wrong side, position it so that the side you want to be on the inside of the card is facing up. Mark down the centre of the card with a faint pencil line, then score along it with a metal ruler and stylus or knife (see above). Make sure you are working in the direction of the grain. Fold the card over and smooth the outside crease with a bone folder or rounded object. If you don't have a bone folder the back of a plastic ruler will work, provided that it is clean.

Types of folds

There are five types of folds you will need to know for basic cardmaking and scrapbooking purposes.

❶ Reverse folds are used for origami. If you have a point made by folding paper diagonally, push the point down inside your model at an angle.

❷ Gatefolds, used for triptych cards, have two outer panels that fold inwards, often meeting at the centre front of the card.

❸ Accordion folds (or zigzag folds) fold first one way and then the other, just as in an accordion.

❹ Valley folds go downwards, like the dip of a valley.

❺ Peak folds (mountain folds) stick upwards, like a mountain peak.

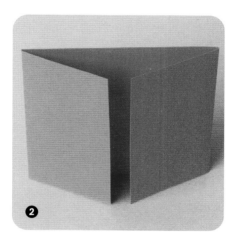

Origami-style envelope

You will need a 21 x 30 cm sheet paper to make an envelope for a 10 x 15 cm card or notelet.

❶ Fold the sheet of paper in half along the length.
❷ Open out flat and fold the top corners of the paper down to the centre crease. The folded sheet will look like a triangular roof on top of a house.
❸ Lay your card to go in the envelope on top, just below the triangle, making sure it is central.
❹ Fold one long side of the paper inwards over the card.
❺ Fold in the other long side and crease, then fold the bottom piece up over the card.
❻ Finally fold the triangular flap down over the card and hold in place with a pretty sticker or decorative fastening.

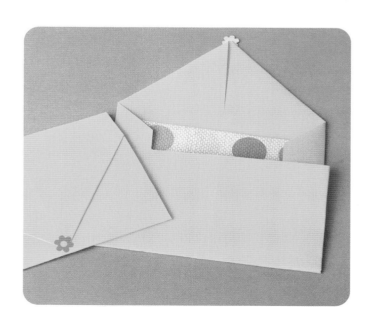

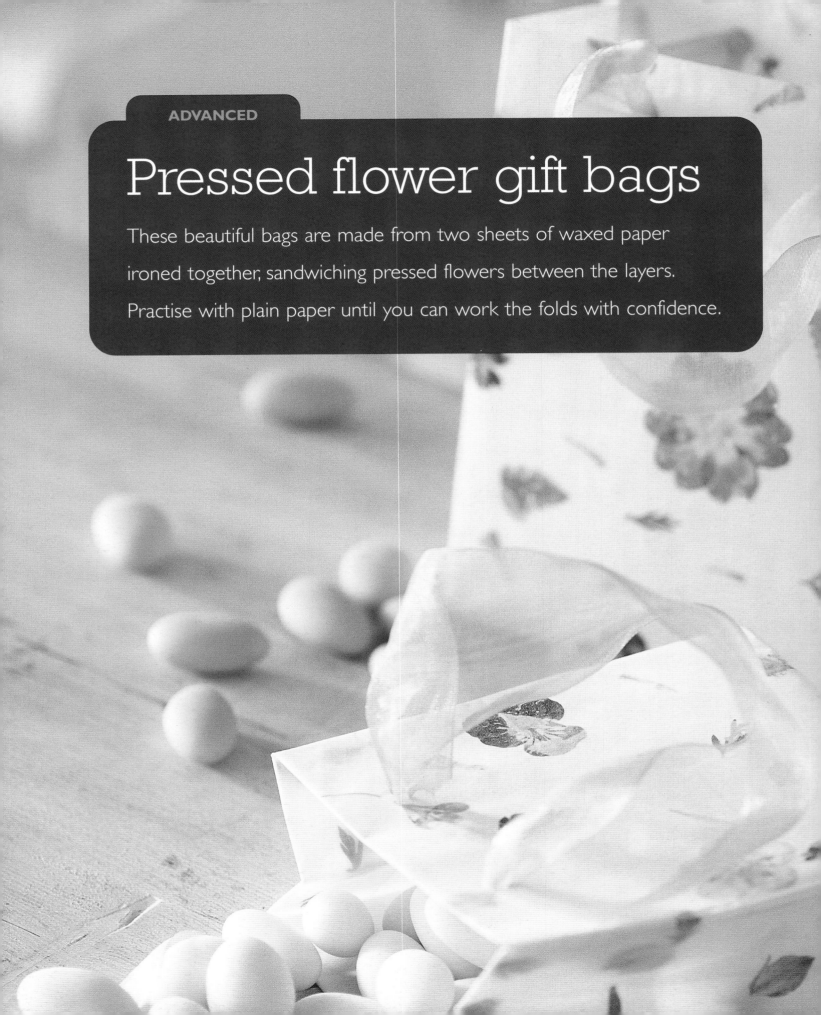

Pressed flower gift bags

These beautiful bags are made from two sheets of waxed paper
ironed together, sandwiching pressed flowers between the layers.
Practise with plain paper until you can work the folds with confidence.

YOU WILL NEED:

- 2 large sheets of waxed paper per bag
- cotton muslin to protect the ironing board
- selection of pressed flowers and leaves
- scissors
- tweezers
- iron
- 2-cm-wide double-sided sticky tape
- hole punch
- cord or organza ribbon for the handle

You will need two 20 x 30 cm sheets of paper for a small bag, two 25 x 43 cm sheets of paper for a medium bag, or two 30 x 52 cm sheets of paper for a large bag.

1 Use an ironing board covered with a piece of muslin for your surface. Place a sheet of waxed paper shiny side up and arrange two or three large flowers on top. Fill in the spaces with smaller flowers and leaves.

2 Once you are satisfied with the arrangement, place the second piece of waxed paper on top, shiny side down. Press the sheet with a cool iron to melt the wax. Be careful not to brown the paper. Allow to cool.

3 Make the sheet into a bag following the diagrams on page 186. Fold the paper in half along the width and open out. At each side of the centre fold, make a fold 3 cm away. This 6-cm-wide area forms the base of the bag. For the bag top, fold over 2 to 4 cm at each short end (Diagram 1).

To form the bag sides, fold over 6 cm along one long edge (Diagram 2). Fold the flap back on itself, exactly in half (Diagram 3). Open out the last fold. Repeat along the other long edge.

Make a diagonal fold between the two 3-cm fold lines on the flap, by folding point A over to point B as is shown in Diagram 4.

Following the photograph, take the end of the fold (1) and place it at the inner corner (2) (Diagram 5). This forms a small triangular flap at the bag base and lifts the second side of the bag into position. Repeat along the other long edge, making sure that the overlap is facing in the same direction on both sides of the bag.

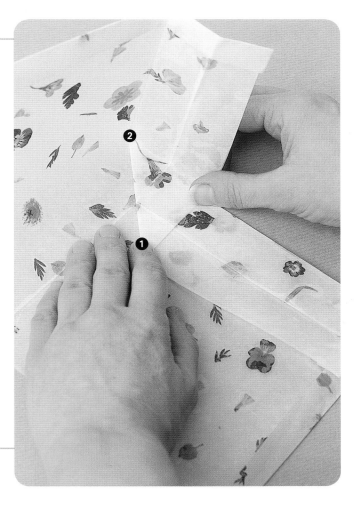

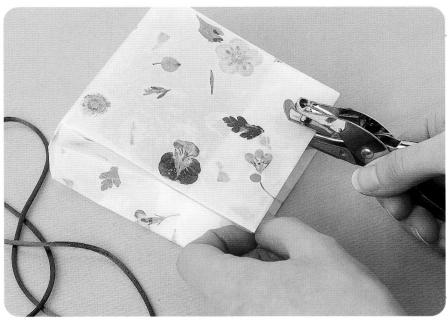

4 Lift the outer flap on each narrow bag side. Stick double-sided tape between the layers of both side panels and under the lifted flap. Stick the top flap over both layers to secure. Re-crease the side seams. Punch two holes, equally spaced, on each side of the bag opening. Finish with cord knotted inside the bag to make the handles.

Origami picture frames

This is a versatile origami frame that can be folded to fit a picture of any size. You don't need to use specialist origami paper – wallpaper has been used here. Any paper thin enough to fold will work well.

YOU WILL NEED:

- wallpaper or sheet of paper
- photograph or picture
- bone folder for creasing the folds (optional)
- decorations such as fabric flowers or brads (optional)

For a 9 x 10 cm photograph you will need a sheet or strip of paper 21 x 30 cm.

1 Fold the paper in half lengthways (down the length of the paper) and crease well; fold in half widthways, then open out both folds.

2 Working from the centre of the paper, bring the right half of the widthways crease down to meet the lower half of the lengthways crease, as shown below. Crease to make a diagonal fold line. Repeat with the left-hand half of the widthways crease.

Rotate the paper 180° and repeat the process, bringing both sides of the widthways crease down to the lengthways crease to make diagonal folds. There should now be 8 fold lines running out of the centre point.

Re-fold the paper in half widthways, tucking the widthways folds inside to meet the lengthways crease. You should form a triangle shape (see step 3).

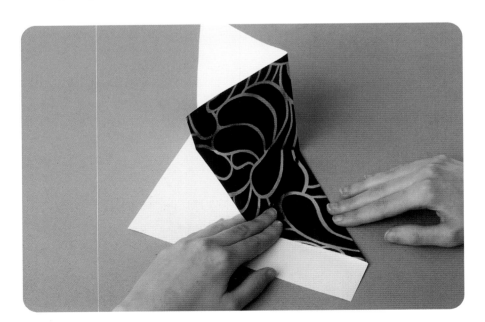

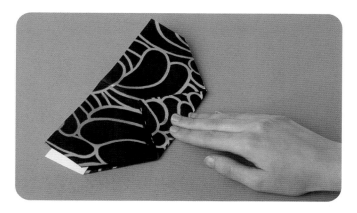

3 Fold the tip of the point inwards to where the corners meet on the inside. (You may need to mark this point on the outside with a pencil to guide you.) Turn the paper over.

4 Pull up the top straight edge to open. Two flaps on the inside will lift up. Open these out and squash them flat to create two triangles.

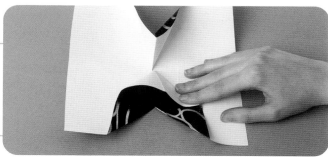

5 Place the picture you wish to frame into the centre. Fold the two straight edges over the picture and crease. (Aim to create a snug fit so that the picture won't be able to slip about.) Remove the picture and remake the folds.

6 Place the picture back in the centre, on top of the folded-over paper. Fold the ends inwards, over the picture. Remove the picture and refold.

7 Slot the picture into the corners of the frame. If desired, finish the frame with a fabric flower or two, a brad or other decoration. The flap at the back of the frame forms a convenient stand whether the picture is landscape or portrait format.

Travel journal

Make this exquisite Eastern-inspired journal to keep the memories of your trip abroad safe. The book is folded to create a number of pockets to store your precious postcards, photographs and tickets.

1 Practise the following stamping technique on a scrap of paper first. As you work, mask sections of the stamps and areas of your stamping with small torn pieces of mulberry paper to create a worn look. When inking the stamp, occasionally press the stamp onto the ink pad at an angle so that not all of the stamp is inked. As you begin stamping the sheet of washi paper, work in blocks of 3 x 2. Continue stamping in a rough pattern until the sheet is full.

2 When the sheet is completely covered leave to dry. Once dry, spray adhesive on the reverse and glue to a sheet of red mulberry paper to form the lining. If necessary, trim the mulberry paper to size.

YOU WILL NEED:

- large sheet of washi paper in a neutral colour
- red mulberry paper slightly larger than the washi sheet
- three medium-size rubber stamps and black ink pad
- spray adhesive
- scissors
- bone folder
- black sealing wax, safety lighter and tinfoil
- stamp or coin to press into the wax seal
- 1 m of red cord or ribbon
- strong glue

For a 14 x 20 cm book you will need a 55 x 80 cm sheet of washi paper. Alternatively, use a 30 x 42 cm sheet to make a mini book.

3 A series of folds and creases turn the flat piece of paper into a book. Firstly, fold the sheet in half widthways so that the red paper is inside. Then unfold and fold in half lengthways so that the sheet is quartered. Fold the long folded edge over to meet the long edges; unfold. Crease all the folds using a bone folder. The sheet is now divided into 8 long sections.

With the paper folded along the width only (with the red paper inside), take the folded edge over to meet the opposite edges of the paper so that the whole sheet of paper is divided into 16 equal portions. Repeat to form the creases on the reverse side of the paper.

4 With the paper folded along the width only, bring the short unfolded edges together, so that the paper is in quarters with four sections showing. Hold the longer folded edge toward you and cut from the spine to the centre fold.

Inexpensive stamps

You can buy rubber stamps in inexpensive sheet form. Cut around the design and mount each one on a clear acrylic block. Glue the back of the stamp to the block with strong glue or use double-sided tape if you want to use them temporarily.

Using stamps

The best way to rubber stamp is by standing up at a table. Standing allows you to put more pressure onto the stamp. Use a scrap of cloth to wipe around the edges of the stamping block. When you have finished stamping, rinse your stamps under the tap with washing up liquid and blot to dry.

5 Open the paper out so that it is only folded along the width. Fold the folded edge over lengthways so that the slits are at the top. Hold each side and push together so that the slit opens up. Push it flat. This gives you four panels, all meeting at the middle like a carousel.

6 Fold the front and back cover around to form the book. Decorate the front of the book with red cord and sealing wax. To avoid ruining your book with unruly wax, make the seal on tinfoil first. Light the wax and let it drip onto the tinfoil. When you have a big enough blob press a small rubber stamp, coin or other small embossed item into the hot wax. Leave to cool before removing the item. Peel the wax away from the tinfoil or cut around it. If you are using coloured wax, try inking the item before pressing it into the wax to create a two-coloured seal. Wind red cord around the book and glue the wax seal over the centre of the cord using strong glue.

CUTTING

The basic tools of the trade are a sharp knife, ruler and cutting mat, plus a pair of paper scissors and perhaps a paper punch or two. As you experiment further you may want to invest in a trimmer or guillotine for cutting straight edges on cards and scrapbooking pages, a shape-cutting or die-cutting system and a growing collection of punches and scissors to embellish your projects.

Basic cutting with scissors

The easiest way to cut paper and card is with a large pair of sharp scissors. Use them just for papercrafting and keep a separate pair for cutting fabric. The best way to cut neatly is to draw a light pencil guideline and follow it with the bottom arm of the scissors.

Cutting with decorative shears can produce some great effects (see page 30–33). You will need to match the patterned edge when taking a second cut to maintain the shaping. This is a great way to create mats for your scrapbooking images and background papers for cards.

Cutting corners

Use small, sharp scissors to help negotiate tricky angles. If you are cutting around the point of a 'V' shape, snip up to the point first and then cut around the rest of the outline. If you are cutting into the 'V', cut into the point twice – do not try to turn the scissors round after the first cut. You may find it easier to trim away most of the waste paper first with larger scissors, and then switch to the smaller blades to cut out the shape precisely.

Cutting circles

One of the most difficult things to cut accurately is a circle. You can buy circle cutters, which are basically a blade and a circular stencil or you can cut your own circles with large scissors. Open the scissors as wide as possible and try to cut around as much of the circle as possible in a single sweep. If you need to make more than one cut, make sure you consistently start with the scissors wide open, so that you make as few cuts as possible. Work slowly, and try to feed the paper into the scissors rather than moving the scissors around the paper.

Cutting with a craft knife

The easiest way to cut a straight line is with a paper trimmer or guillotine. If you have not yet invested in one, you will get a professional finish from a craft knife, metal ruler and cutting mat. When cutting with a craft knife, always follow a pencil guide line. It also helps to stand up to create enough pressure. Use the lines on the mat to position the card or paper. Line the ruler up on the biggest area of card (it is less likely to slip). Bring the knife in so that it is resting against the ruler. Press down firmly with the knife and cut down the line in a single, fluid motion. Make another cut if necessary – do not release pressure on the ruler until you are satisfied with the cut. This will prevent you having to realign your work.

Cutting curves

Curves require a firm, swift motion. It is best to cut shapes in one go rather than stop and start, as this will create a jagged edge. Follow a pencil line and press down consistently with quite a strong pressure to get an accurate cut. Move your whole body around the shape rather than just your hand. If you stop, continue cutting from where you left off. As when using scissors, it is best to move the paper rather than the blade, if you can.

Cutting thick card or mountboard

Use a guillotine or trimmer where possible, and if not use a steel ruler, craft knife and cutting mat. Stand up and apply plenty of pressure to cut through the thickness.

Care with knives
Never put knives down without replacing the safety cap or returning them to a case. Craft knives or scalpels should be kept as sharp as possible – a blunt knife is more likely to slip than a sharp one. They are not for children.

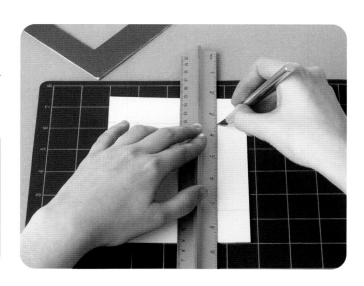

Punching

Punches are available in millions of different shapes and sizes. They are a fast, clean and efficient way to cut holes and create embellishments. Press the punch button down with your thumb on a small punch, or with your whole palm on the larger sizes. Use a single firm motion – it should cut through easily in one movement. To sharpen the punch, cut a few shapes out of thin embossing foil.

Making holes for brads

Use a craft knife to make a small incision for the arms of the brad to go through. Mark on the position first and make your hole at the mark. Push the brad through and open out the arms on the back to secure it. Don't worry if you can't make the hole quite as neatly as you'd like because the brad will cover it. Alternatively, use a small hole punch or plier punch to make the hole for the brad (see page 82–83).

Making holes for eyelets

To make a hole for an eyelet use a hole punch or plier punch. If you want to make a hole in the centre of a piece of card or paper you will need a specialist eyelet tool and a small hammer.

Punched confetti

Keep the punched-out shapes and use them as table confetti at your next party.

Mexican candles

Inspired by the cut-paper art developed in Mexico, brightly coloured candles will light up every room in your house. These altar-style candles would look excellent grouped in different colours around a hearth.

YOU WILL NEED:

- tissue paper in assorted colours
- large candles, approximately 14 x 22 cm
- tracing paper
- pencil
- stapler and staples
- cutting mat and craft knife
- scissors and pinking shears
- paper punches with assorted shapes to cut intricate border designs
- spray adhesive
- newspaper
- clear candle-making wax
- shallow baking tin approximately 25 x 18 cm or to fit your candles

1 Place six layers of tissue paper together and trace the template (see page 187) onto the top sheet. Staple the tissue sheets together, placing the staples in areas that will be cut away.

2 On a cutting mat, and using a craft knife or small pair of scissors, cut away the negative spaces in the pattern. Cut out the areas without staples in them first so the papers hold together for as long as possible. Trim around the edges and then cut out the stapled areas in the pattern last.

3 Separate the sheets of tissue. Spray the back of each one lightly with adhesive and stick all the layers together. Lay the layers out flat and apply spray adhesive to the top surface. Lay a candle lengthways across the edge of the design.

  Roll the candle along the cut paper until the two edges meet with a slight overlap. With the staple in an open position, staple along the length of the seam, putting staples lengthways along the overlapped edges. If you plan to make more than one candle, prepare all candles to this stage.

4 Cover the bottom of a tray with clear wax. Place the tray on the top of a stove and melt the wax over a medium heat. Never leave hot wax unattended. Gently lay the candle in the tray of melted wax, putting the seam-side down first. Carefully, holding the candle at both ends, roll it in the melted wax to coat the tissue paper. Take the candle out of the melted wax and stand it on old newspaper to harden. Repeat for all the candles, topping up the melted wax as the level goes down.

Burning tip

By using large church candles you can gently roll down the edges of the tissue paper as the candle burns and melts the wax in the middle. Although there is very little danger with this technique, never leave lit candles unattended.

Shelf border

This attractive border is made with top-quality artist's watercolour paper. Here, a simple eyelet punch has been used to create a lacy pattern, but you may wish to experiment with different punches.

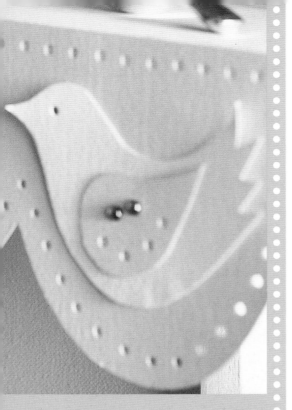

YOU WILL NEED:

- card or template plastic
- tinted artist's watercolour paper in white or grey and warm cream (or see the tip opposite)
- tape measure
- pencil
- craft knife
- cutting mat
- scissors
- hole punch
- small paper fasteners/brads
- glue or double-sided tape

1 Create a template from the border design on page 186, using card or template plastic. Measure the length of the shelf. Draw around the template to transfer it to white or grey watercolour paper, repeating the design until it is the length required for the shelf. Cut out the watercolour paper. Now punch out the holes marked on your template so you can transfer the hole positions to your paper. Transfer the hole positions to the scalloped edge and then the top edge, as shown.

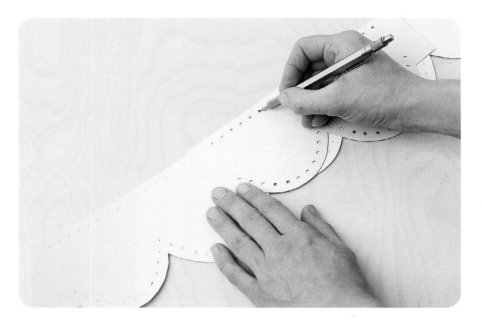

2 Use your hole punch to make the holes in your paper shelf liner. The punch shown below is an eyelet punch that creates different sized holes. If you use one of these make sure the hole size is consistent.

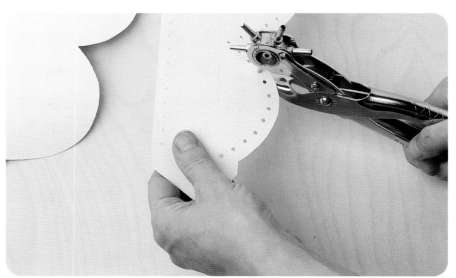

3 Transfer the bird, wing and flower pieces from page 186 onto card or template plastic and cut out. Punch the holes in the templates as indicated. Place the large flower template on cream watercolour paper, draw around it and cut out. Use the same technique to mark and cut the flower centres from white or grey paper and the birds from cream paper. Cut half the required birds with the template facing one way, then turn it over and cut the rest. Cut the wings from white or grey paper. Punch holes in the wings and the bird as indicated.

4 Hold the wing in position on each bird and push paper fasteners or plain brads through the holes. Position the birds on the border above the large curves. Push the fasteners through the border and open out on the reverse side. Fix the flowers in the same way above the small curves. Attach the border to the edge of the shelf with glue or double-sided tape.

Colour tip

If you don't have several shades of watercolour paper, cut all the pieces in white and then tint them with a watercolour paint wash.

Water lilies

Make a flotilla of lilies as a table decoration. With the help of a few candles you can waterproof the flowers so they will happily come into contact with water. Chalks add subtle shading.

YOU WILL NEED:

- dark green pearly paper
- white pearly paper
- scissors
- pencil
- two tealight candles
- bain-marie or saucepan and heatproof bowl for melting wax
- unwanted spoon
- chalks

1 Cut a lily pad and set of petals using the templates on page 185. Draw the petals onto white pearly paper and the lily pad onto the green paper. You will need to cut three concentric sets of petals for each flower, the largest is 10 cm in diameter and the smallest 4.5 cm. Cut out the leaf and petals.

2 Shade the centres of the petals with chalks. Make the larger set darker by applying wet chalk. Graduate the shading on the petals so that they get lighter towards the centre. Shade the centre piece (smallest flower) with yellow chalk. Add veins to the lily pad with wet green chalk.

3   Pinch the tip of each petal and fold it at the base by bending it forward. Work your way around all the petals pinching and bending to make the flower more three-dimensional.

4   Take two tealight candles and remove them from their metal cases. Pull out the wicks and metal tab as well. Melt the wax over water in a bain-marie. Dip the largest set of petals into the melted wax to coat it. Use a metal spoon to retrieve it. Leave the wax to cool on the petals. Next take the centre set of petals and dip into the wax. While cooling hold the petals closed to form a bud. The hardened wax will seal the petals closed.

5   Screw up the lily pad into a ball to create texture. Smooth it out flat and dip in the melted wax as before.

6   Stick all the pieces together by dipping the round base of the petals into the wax. Hold the petals closed by their tips and dip the bases into the hot wax. Work from the largest set to the smallest, pressing together the waxed bases as you go.

Japanese hanging

This lovely blind is made from a combination of strong tissue paper and Japanese lace paper, though you could use any Japanese paper of your choice. You may need several sheets, depending on the size of the blind.

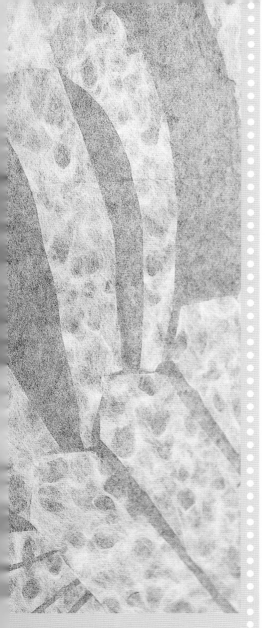

1 If you want to make the hanging as a blind for a small window, measure your window, taking into account whether you want the blind to hang inside or outside the window's recess. Cut graph paper to this exact size, joining pieces as necessary. Mark out nine squares in a 3 x 3 grid on the graph paper (to match the template on page 187). Using a pencil, carefully copy the template from page 187 onto the graph paper, square by square, to create an enlarged version of the design. Trace the shapes onto your Japanese paper with intermittent soft pencil lines. Cut the design out, just inside the lines.

YOU WILL NEED:

- Japanese paper, such as lace paper
- strong tissue paper
- large sheet(s) of graph paper
- soft pencil
- ruler or tape measure
- spray adhesive
- fusible bonding web
- two wooden or bamboo poles for hanging

Japanese paper

There are plenty of Japanese papers available today, many of them variations of washi paper, which is strong, flexible, absorbent and lightweight. Lace paper is ideal because of its translucency, or try angel hair paper, which contains stranded fibres or ayanishiki, which is flecked with gold. All true washi papers are naturally acid-free so you can use your leftovers for scrapbooking.

2 As a backing for the Japanese-paper shapes, cut nine pieces of strong tissue paper the size of the squares on your graph paper. Lay them out in order and stick the Japanese paper pieces centrally on top, following the graph-paper template. Set these aside.

To make a backing for the hanging, cut out another nine squares of strong tissue paper to the size of the squares on the graph paper, this time adding the following allowances to each one: for the centre square add 5 mm all round; for the remaining squares add 5 cm to the outside edge(s) and 5 mm to the inside edges. For example, for a corner square add 5 cm to the two outer edges and 5 mm to the remaining two edges. The remaining squares will have one outside edge that has the 5-cm allowance added to it, and three edges with the 5-mm allowance added.

3 Mark and cut 5-mm-wide strips of fusible bonding web. Working in rows across the backing pieces, iron a strip of bonding web to the joining edges of the tissue paper. Peel off the backing paper from the web and iron the next panel in position, overlapping the paper by 1 cm. When you have made the three rows of the backing, join the rows together in the same way. Lay the backing face down on the graph paper and line up the seams between the marked lines. Spray the front of the decorated squares, and stick them face down onto the framework of the hanging. (You will need to reverse the layout so that the squares are in the correct position when the hanging is turned over to the right side.) Fold over the 5-cm hem allowance all round the backing and open out. Cut 5-cm-wide lengths of Japanese paper and stick them along the edges of the hanging, between the corner squares. Spray the hem and fold it over, cutting away the corners to reduce bulk.

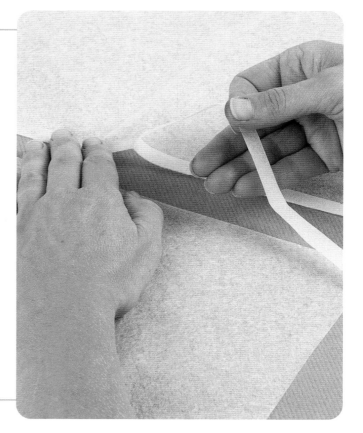

4 To make the tabs, cut out fourteen 8 x 25 cm pieces of strong tissue paper and spray on one side with adhesive. Fold the paper into three, mask the strips, and spray the last 5 cm of each end.

5 Fix seven tabs, equally spaced, along the top and bottom edges of the design. Hang using a thin wooden or bamboo pole threaded through each row of tabs.

Christmas box

Make this festive box to store your decorations safely when you take them down from the tree. Use paper with a high shine, but be careful with the glue, as shiny paper will show marks more easily.

YOU WILL NEED:

- round hat box
- metallic spray paint
  (optional)
- card or template plastic
- Selection of three
  Christmassy papers, cut to
  the circumference and
  height of the box (one
  decorative paper for the
  background and two plain
  colours for the silhouettes)
- soft pencil
- cutting knife and self-healing
  cutting mat
- spray adhesive or stick glue

1   If the interior of your box or the lid are not a suitable colour or design, use spray paint to cover it. Use two thin coats of paint rather than one thick coat, which will run, leaving it to dry after each application.

2   Copy or trace the designs on page 184 to make templates out of thick card or template plastic. Cut out your templates and draw round them onto your two papers for the silhouettes, moving each template along and turning it over to make a scene that fits the full width of the paper.

3 Cut out the two scenes with a craft knife and cutting mat, using a different paper for each one. You may find it helpful to cut away the bulk of waste paper and make a rough outline first. Cut from the edges into the centre, as the centre is the weakest point. (See page 74 for some helpful advice on cutting with a knife.)

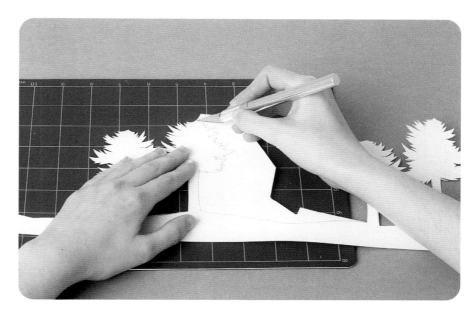

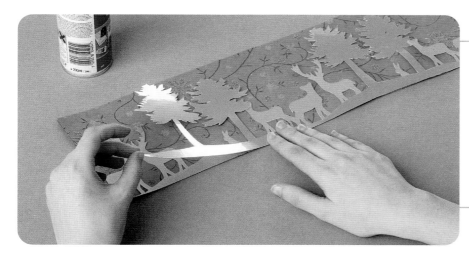

4 Stick the two scenes onto the background Christmas paper, one at a time, using spray adhesive or stick glue.

5 Once the glue has dried, spray the box with glue or apply plenty of glue from a glue stick. Roll the box along the back of the background paper, keeping the edges of the paper level with the edges of the box as you go. Once the glue has dried, your storage box is now complete and ready to use.

DÉCOUPAGE

The term 'découpage' derives from the French word *découper*, meaning to cut out. Découpage flourished in Europe during the 18th and 19th centuries, and many elaborate examples remain in existence. Craftsmen produced beautiful boxes and chests that were made to look like they were hand painted – an effect made by applying many thin layers of varnish to the finished piece until it was glassy smooth.

Cut-outs

Pictures can be cut from magazines, books, wallpaper, wrapping paper, photographs, napkins and specially made prints. Lightweight papers are better suited for découpage. Very thin papers can be sealed before cutting out to strengthen them and stop the edges from curling. Use découpage medium following the manufacturer's instructions, or PVA glue diluted with two parts water. Apply the medium or diluted PVA to the cut-outs with a brush and allow to dry. To keep the brush in good condition, wash it well after use with soapy water.

Choosing paper

Avoid embossed and textured papers or very thin glossy paper. Some images can smudge when you smooth them down. If in doubt, test the paper first. Always have a few spare copies of the images you plan to use, just in case a mistake is made.

Preparing cut-outs

When découpaging with pictures, cut them out following the exact line around the edge of the image. Use a pair of sharp scissors with short blades that are dedicated only to cutting paper or card. Use straight scissors for straight edges and curved scissors on angles and shaped edges. Alternatively, use a craft knife and cutting mat. Hold the scissors and cut around the image anticlockwise if you are right-handed and clockwise if you are left-handed. Feed the paper through the scissors with a smooth motion, keeping the hand holding the scissors still. If white edges appear then hold the scissors or knife at a slight angle to give a bevelled effect.

Preparing the item

Wood, cardboard, metal, ceramics and even candles can be découpaged but they should all be properly prepared to give the best results. Ensure that the item is clean and smooth before you begin. Fine sandpaper can be used to make a smooth surface, while mild detergent works well for cleaning. Porous objects, such as wood, need to be sealed beforehand, using either varnish or a sealant such as diluted PVA glue or with a coat of paint.

A variety of paint effects can be used to prepare the surface before the images are pasted on, including sponging, marbling and distressing. If you wish to use a crackle medium, apply this as a last coat, after the images have been secured in place.

Three-dimensional découpage

Three-dimensional découpage involves layering the image to achieve physical depth. Several copies of the image are needed and the top layers are shaped slightly to enhance the effect.

Place the image in the palm of your hand and rub it in a circular motion, using a shaping tool or the back of a tea-spoon or a pen lid. This will make the edges curl upwards. Depending on which way the image needs to be shaped, it can be rubbed face up or face down.

Study the picture and decide which areas recede and which protrude. When selecting images, ensure that there are definite lines and areas of depth to make the process easier. Flowers are a popular subject.

Use silicone adhesive to apply the layers, or foam pads if you prefer. When using silicone adhesive, allow each layer to dry before adding the next. Protect the top layers with a coat of découpage medium or varnish to finish.

Stickers

There are a range of stickers available to use for découpage. These include clear, vellum, three-dimensional stickers and transfers. Try using clear stickers or transfers to decorate a candle for a special occasion, and finish with a coat of découpage medium. Three-dimensional stickers will add instant glamour to cards and scrapbook pages.

Layering tip
Rubber stamps are an easy way to produce three-dimensional images. Simply stamp the image several times to create the layers.

Collage

Collage is a form of découpage, but rather than just simple paper images, other items are introduced such as plain papers, tickets, photographs and other memorabilia. Three-dimensional embellishments such as buttons, shells and ribbon can also be added. The effects can be stunning – this technique is often used to create scrapbook pages and journals (see the album cover on page 108), and will work just as well with greetings cards and memory boxes.

Applying the cut-outs

Once you have prepared the surface and cut-outs, arrange the images on the object, moving them around until you are pleased with the effect. Use a paintbrush to apply découpage medium or glue to the object's surface. Do not apply glue or paste to the cut-out, as this will stretch it.

Alternatively, use a special spray adhesive that can be applied directly onto the paper. Use an old shoebox lined with scrap paper or a plastic bag to protect the surroundings, as shown. Place the image face down in the box and spray the back lightly with adhesive.

Use a clean cloth to smooth the cut-outs in place. Allow to dry thoroughly before applying a thin layer of varnish or découpage medium to finish. Add one or more further coats as needed.

Japanese vases

One of the most delightful crafts in Japan is the art of gift-wrapping. Beautiful boxes are tied and finished with exquisite gift tags. Here, a simple bamboo container is tied with a decorative label and raffia.

YOU WILL NEED:

- bamboo vase
- 30-cm square of corrugated paper
- scissors
- double-sided sticky tape
- PVA glue solution (diluted with five parts water)
- white tissue paper
- small sponge
- plain Japanese origami paper
- patterned origami paper
- white shoji paper or other handmade paper
- medium-sized Japanese paintbrush
- black ink
- natural raffia, paper string, or ribbon

1 Measure and cut a strip of corrugated paper to the same height as the vase, so that the grooves run horizontally around it. Wrap the corrugated paper around the vase. Crease and mark the point where the paper overlaps, and cut along the line. Stick the corrugated paper snugly around the vase with double-sided sticky tape at the join.

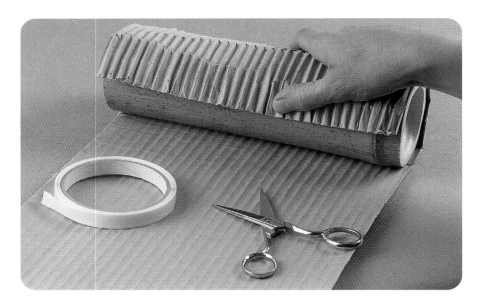

2 Tear the tissue paper into long, thin, irregular pieces. Dip the sponge into the glue solution and paste the tissue pieces onto the corrugated paper around the vase, working the tissue paper into the flutes. Allow the vase to dry overnight, away from direct heat.

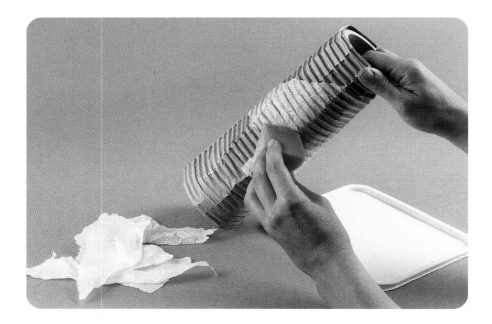

3 Cut a rectangle of plain origami paper and a slightly smaller rectangle of patterned origami paper to make a label for the front of the vase. Cut a piece of shoji paper slightly smaller still. Use the Japanese brush and ink to draw motifs to resemble Japanese script on the shoji paper, as shown.

Bamboo vase
You can make your own bamboo vase by cutting a thick length of bamboo just below one of its joints (where the bamboo bulges).

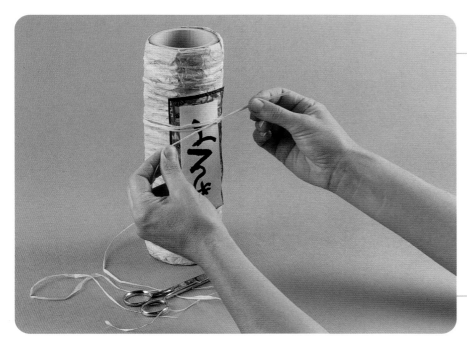

4 Stick the patterned origami paper centrally on the plain origami paper rectangle and when the painted shoji paper is dry, stick it centrally on top to complete the label. Tie the label in position on the front of the vase with natural raffia or ribbon, as shown.

Jewellery box

Fairy wrapping paper decorates this lovely jewellery box with funky modern motifs. By changing the paper and the box colour you use, you can create whatever effect you like.

YOU WILL NEED:

- readymade jewellery box
- sandpaper
- emulsion paint and brush (optional)
- small, sharp scissors or craft knife and cutting mat
- wrapping paper with motifs of your choice
- PVA glue or découpage medium
- silicone adhesive
- paintbrush
- fabric flowers (optional)

1 Prepare the box by gently sanding it. Paint it, if desired, and leave to dry then sand again. Wipe clean. Roughly cut out the motifs from your sheet of paper and apply a thin layer of PVA glue mixed with two parts water (or découpage medium) to the back. Allow to dry.

2 When the paper is dry, trim the shapes precisely using small sharp scissors or a craft knife. If the design has many curves you may find it easiest to use curved scissors on these areas.

3 Use the glue or découpage medium to stick the images to the box, applying the glue to the box rather than the paper. (If you do it the other way around the paper may stretch.) It does not matter if not all of the glue is covered by the paper motifs – several layers of glue will be added to the entire surface at the next stage and these will cover any current glue marks.

4 When the glue is dry, apply very thin layers of the glue or découpage medium over the entire surface. Leave to dry and then sand lightly. Repeat the 'varnishing' process, applying enough coats to achieve the desired effect of a smooth finish. Fabric flowers can be stuck onto the box to add a three-dimensional effect, if desired.

Family-tree album

Create a long-lasting memento of your family past and present with this beautiful photograph album designed around a family tree. Add more colourful touches for contemporary-style pictures.

YOU WILL NEED:

- photograph album or scrapbook
- sheet of paper large enough to cover your album unless it is already suitably covered
- card or template plastic
- soft pencil
- scissors or craft knife and cutting mat
- square of Japanese lace paper at least the size of the album cover
- strips of handmade and scrapbook papers
- photographs
- metal embellishments and paper daisies
- acid-free glue
- double-sided tape (optional)

1 Unless your album already has a suitable paper cover, recover it with coordinating paper. Chose a selection of photographs and collage items for the decorations.

2 Trace the tree shape from page 188 onto card or template plastic and cut it out with a craft knife and mat or using small scissors. Transfer the design onto Japanese lace paper and cut it out.

3 Cut strips of coordinating papers and arrange them on the cover towards the bottom of the album. Stick the papers in place then stick the tree shape on top, as shown.

4 Arrange the photographs and collage items onto the album cover until you are pleased with the effect. Use a suitable glue or double-sided sticky tape to fix the items to the cover. Acid-free papers and adhesives will ensure that the album is archival safe. (Scrapbooking papers and washi papers, including lace paper, are acid-free.)

ROLLING

Rolling is a simple method of giving paper added dimension. You can either roll freehand, turning the paper around itself or you can curl it around a cylindrical item such as a cocktail stick, pencil or quilling tool. Rolls can be loosely or precisely coiled. They can be shaped before rolling them by trimming into triangles or afterwards by pinching and tweaking them.

Basic rolls

The easiest rolls are made from straight strips of paper. The strip can be folded to make a fatter roll or left flat. Turn one of the shorter edges in on itself and roll the strip around itself. For an even roll, work on a flat, level surface, such as a tabletop, or for a rougher effect, roll the paper strips in you hands.

Beads from shaped rolls

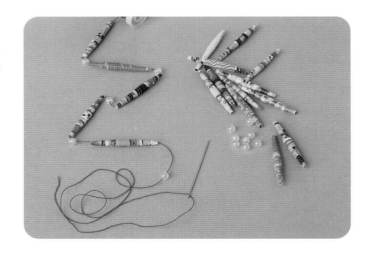

Rolled triangles make great beads. An isosceles triangle will create a bead with a raised centre, while an equilateral triangle will create a flatter bead. The width of the triangle's base is equal to the finished width of the bead, while the length of the triangle determines how fat the bead will be.

Cut out your triangle and spray glue on the back. Now start rolling the base around a cocktail stick or toothpick. Make sure you start off evenly otherwise the middle of the bead will be off centre. Roll flat on a tabletop for neat results. When you reach the pointed end add a dab of PVA glue and roll the end closed. Paint the base and/or tip of the triangle for a decorative effect.

Decorative beads

To embellish your paper beads you can either paint the paper before you start, as shown above, or use decorative paper including origami paper, magazine pages, wrapping paper and wallpaper.

To give your beads a more durable and attractive finish, coat them with clear acrylic varnish, PVA glue or even coloured nail varnish. Thread them with a long darning needle. They look particularly effective with a round bead strung between them to set off the colours.

Quilling

Quilling is the art of rolling very thin strips of paper to create delicate embellishments. It is an old technique dating back to the Renaissance and is traditionally used for making flowers to decorate cards or create pictures. Although quilling has something of an old-fashioned image it need not be dull or stuffy. To bring it into the 21st century, experiment with the techniques and produce something altogether different.

Quilling paper can be bought in pre-cut strips, normally in a multi-colour pack. The width of the strips can vary but it is generally 5 mm. Tools (which have a prong in the middle for you to wind the paper on) can be bought inexpensively from larger craft stores. Or you can buy paper strips and a tool together in a kit form.

Quilling is easy to do, if a little time-consuming, and involves turning the paper strip tightly around a quilling tool to make a spiral.

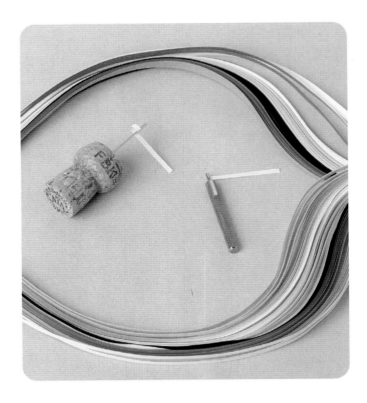

Quilling on a budget

Make your own quilling tool from a darning needle and a cork. Cut the top off the darning needle with wire cutters or strong scissors and smooth down the edges with sandpaper. Push the needle into a cork and you have a cheap yet functional quilling tool.

Shredding paper

Paper can be cut into thin strips with the aid of an office paper shredder. This will allow you to make your own quilling strips in whatever colour you desire – dayglow, metallic, patterned or even from newsprint.

Gluing quills

To glue quills shut you can either glue a straight end or tear it before gluing to make the join invisible. Quills can be glued onto card and paper with PVA or stronger clear glue. If you want to protect the life of the quills you could spray them with clear varnish.

Basic shapes

Use strands of pre-bought quilling paper or cut your own narrow strips from your chosen paper, using different widths to create shapes of varying depths.

To make the basic loose coil (top), insert one end of the paper in the quilling tool and wrap the paper around on itself. Guide the paper strip with one hand and turn the tool with the other. Try to keep an even tension and wrapping speed. When you reach the end, remove the coil and leave it to unwind and settle.

To make a closed coil (bottom left), work as above, but glue the end closed after the coil has unwound to the required degree.

To make a tight peg (centre), roll the paper as tightly as possible, remove from the tool and hold shut with one hand. Add a dab of glue to the end of the paper with the other hand and press closed to secure it.

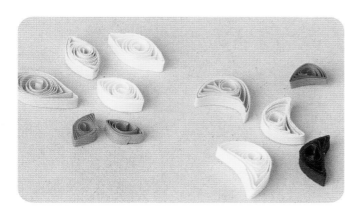

Eyes and moons

To make a teardrop or eye shape, first make a closed coil. Pinch both ends with thumb and forefinger for an eye shape or just one end for a teardrop.

To make a crescent moon shape, make a closed coil and use the end of the quilling tool or a round pencil to press into the coil. Push the two ends of the coil around it to create the crescent shape.

Experimental shapes

- Square: make an eye-shape and pinch it again in opposite corners to complete the shape.
- Heart: fold a strip in half and quill both ends.
- 'S'-shaped curly quill: roll one end of the strip one way and roll the other end the other way. There are plenty of other shapes you could make. Have fun experimenting with shapes such as fish, birds, leaves, stars or even numbers.

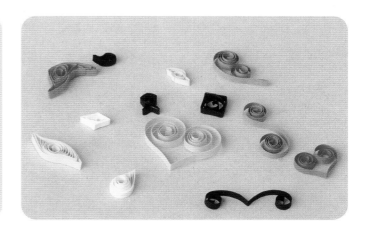

Quilled box lid

Quilling can be as outrageous as you want it to be. This box lid, for example, has been decorated with a bold combination of metallic and fluorescent papers for an effect that cannot go unnoticed.

YOU WILL NEED:

- round box blank with lid approximately 15 cm in diameter
- white office paper
- pack of fluorescent office paper
- silver spray paint
- old cardboard box and newspaper
- pencil
- paper shredder
- quilling tool
- PVA glue

1 Spray the circular box silver, using one or two thin coats of paint for an even coverage. Spray it inside an old cardboard box to stop the paint travelling and protect the surrounding area with newspaper. Spray both sides of a sheet of white paper too, leaving the paint to dry after each coat.

2 When the paint on the box lid is completely dry, use your pencil to draw a rough spiral pattern on top with four 'C'-shaped arcs, and mark on a circle for the centre.

3 Shred the sheet of silver paper, trying to shred it evenly so the strips will be straight. Shred four sheets of fluorescent paper in green, orange, yellow and pink as well.

Making quills
When making quills for a project, always make a few more than you need, so that when you start gluing, you won't have to stop to make more halfway through.

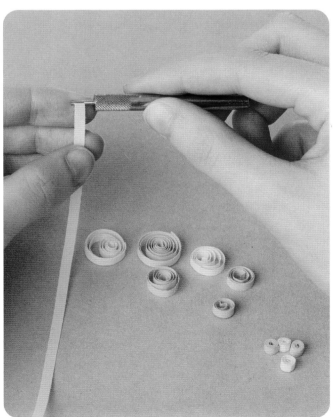

4 Using a quilling tool, start making pegs. Make at least 20 green, 15 yellow, 10 orange and 5 pink pegs. Make 12 different-sized green closed coils starting small then getting larger, making the largest coil about 2.5 cm wide. Make another matching set, so you have 24 green coils. This will form the outer band.

Make 10 different-sized yellow closed quills; make two matching sets. Make 7 different-sized orange quills; make two sets. Make 7 different-sized pink closed end quills. For the centre take a yellow peg and glue a green strip to it. Wrap the green around the yellow to create a two-toned coil.

Glue the quills to the box lid with PVA glue. Start with the outside green ring and work your way to the centre. When you have finished gluing on all the fluorescent quills start making loose silver quills to fit into the gaps (you will need to make about 100, in varying sizes). Attach these as well to finish.

Rock-and-roll cuff

This contemporary bracelet features beads made from decorative Japanese paper. The shirring elastic allows it to stretch over your hand and means it can be worn on different parts of the arm.

YOU WILL NEED:

- sheet of lightweight decorative Japanese paper at least 25 cm long
- gold beads with big holes
- scissors
- spray adhesive
- cocktail stick
- PVA glue
- clear nail varnish or acrylic varnish
- long darning needle
- coloured shirring elastic

To fit a small or medium wrist you'll need 20 rolled beads and 40 gold beads.

Before you start, check that your needle threaded with elastic will fit through the gold beads.

1 Cut 20 isosceles triangles from the Japanese paper. Make them 5 cm wide at the base and 25 cm long, or adapt the size if you want your beads to be smaller or larger than the ones shown.

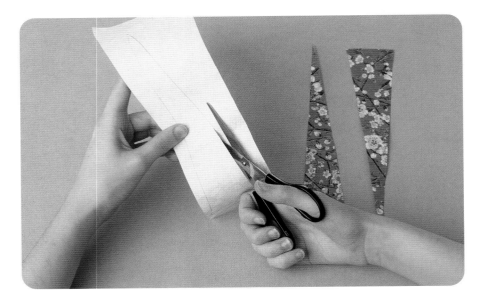

2 Spray glue onto the back of each triangular strip and roll it around a cocktail stick. Glue the pointed end shut with PVA glue. Roll all 20 triangles. Varnish the beads with clear acrylic varnish or nail varnish to protect them and prolong the life of the bracelet.

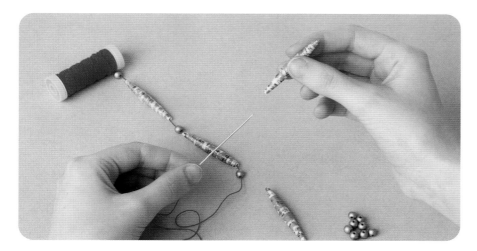

3 Thread a long darning needle with shirring elastic – don't cut the end but keep it attached to the spool. Thread on a gold bead followed by a rolled bead and so on until you have threaded on all 20 rolled beads. Finish with a gold bead.

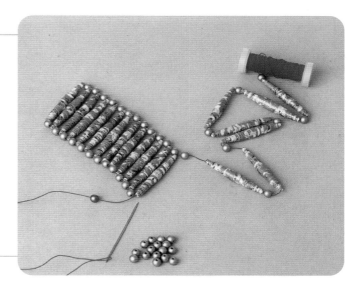

4 Pull the elastic so you have a long thread at the needle end and the beads are up close to the spool. Turn back and thread the needle through the last rolled bead. Pull the needle through and then add a gold bead. Next, go back through the next paper bead on the string, add a gold bead, and then go through the next rolled bead on the string. You are making a figure of eight with the elastic. Pull the elastic tight as you work. Keep threading through the rolled beads and adding a gold bead until you have reached the end.

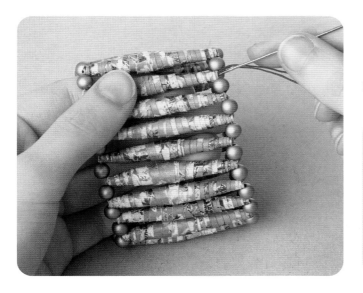

5 Pull the elastic taut and knot the end securely. Add another knot to ensure that the elastic will not come undone. Cut off the tails and push the knot inside the nearest bead to hide it.

Finishing tip
For an easy way to hide the elastic ends, do not trim after knotting. Take the needle back through the final bead, pull tight and trim close to the end of the bead. Once the elastic is released it will stretch back inside the bead, hiding the ends.

Holiday wreath

Paper flowers are very satisfying to make but how can you display your creations to best advantage? A wreath is the ideal solution. Made from festive papers and hung on the door, it is there to welcome all comers.

YOU WILL NEED:

- four 55 x 80 cm sheets of double-sided paper in festive colours
- 35-cm-diameter polystyrene ring or flower foam ring
- scissors
- PVA glue
- glue gun and glue sticks to attach the flowers to the ring
- organza ribbon for hanging

1 Fold a sheet of paper in half widthways. Cut rough strips 2 to 5 cm wide from the paper. Vary the width to make the overall effect look random. Cut the strips in half down the fold. You will need about 80 flowers and each flower requires two strips so cut 160 strips in total.

2 To make the centres for the flower, fold the top edge of a strip over and flatten it. Roll the strip loosely in on itself and glue the end with PVA glue. Vary the centres by making some tighter than others and roll some one side up and some the other way up for more variety. Make 80.

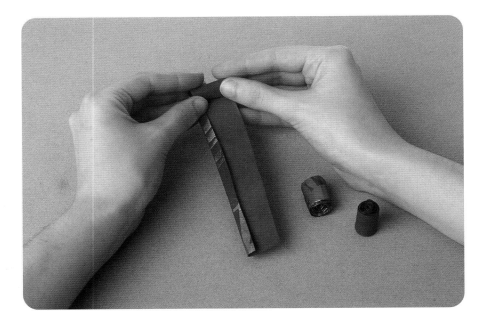

3 Make fringes to form the petals of the flowers by snipping your way along the edge of the remaining strips. Leave a 1-cm band uncut. Cut some fringes with wider spaced snips for variety.

4 Run a line of PVA glue along the uncut part of the fringed strips and wrap one around each flower centre. Glue the end to finish. Once the glue has dried, fan open the petals by pressing the fringed paper back.

5 Cover the polystyrene ring with glue. Wrap leftover strips of paper around it to cover the ring completely. Leave to dry.

6 Glue the flowers to the ring, arranging them randomly for a pleasing effect. Attach ribbon to the back of the ring so you can hang the wreath.

Wreath ring

If you can't find a polystyrene ring you can make your own from a ring of cardboard. Wrap it tightly in newspaper followed by layers of tissue paper to create an even surface.

WEAVING

Weaving is normally associated with textiles but can work equally well with paper – simply cut, tear or fold it into thin strips and get weaving. Paper can also be bought in string and ribbon forms, which make complex weaving possible. You can make your own string by tightly twisting strips of tissue paper and then either weave it or even knit or crochet it together.

Woven paper

Thin paper strips can be woven under and over each other to create a crisscross pattern just as you would on a weaving loom. It's great for making backgrounds for cards and scrapbooking, for embellishment or to make a type of fabric to cover boxes, picture frames, notebooks and more.

Paper ribbons make weaving easy. You can buy them or make your own from paper leftovers – a great way of using up scraps (see page 130).

To experiment you can modify the weaving, perhaps going over two strands then under one, or you could try leaving gaps in the finished weaving or weave with a mixture of paper and fabric strips.

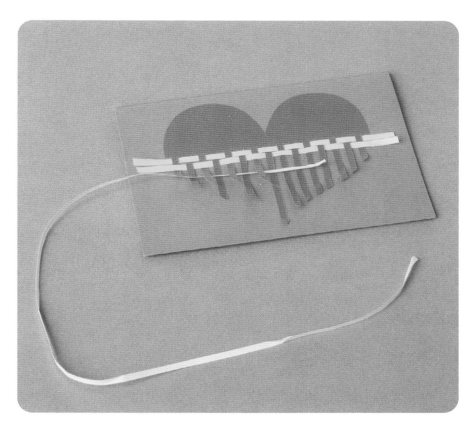

Paper string knitting

Knitting is another form of weaving, using needles rather than a loom. Go crazy and have a go at knitting with paper string. If you don't have any knitting needles try using sharpened pencils. As the string is rigid you will have to knit quite loosely. Use this technique to make jewellery, like the choker being made here. Combine the paper string with some rolled paper beads, or use some bright plastic and glass beads to add colour and sparkle. If you can find some thick paper rope, you could even knit your own paper bag.

Making paper ribbon

You can buy paper ribbon (often used for gift wrapping) or you can make your own from tissue paper. Big packs of single coloured tissue papers can be bought in bundles known as quires. To make your own ribbon cut strips of tissue paper 2.5 cm wide. Spray one side with spray glue and fold the strip in half widthways to make a 12-mm double strip. Fold in half again to create a 6-mm-wide ribbon. Simply glue more folded tissue onto the end of it to elongate it. This can then be used for plaiting.

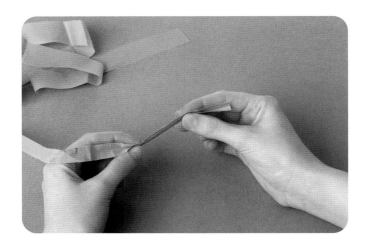

How to plait

Paper ribbon can be woven into plaits and coiled and stitched to create coasters, baskets and cup holders. A simple plait of three strands is effective enough. To plait, tape your three strands of ribbon to a table top and cross the left-hand strand over the middle. Plait the right-hand strand over the strand in the middle. Keep plaitting from the left and then the right, crossing over the middle strand each time to create a rope.

Plaiting tips

• To avoid getting into a tangle when plaiting long strands, keep one strand on one side of your knee and the other two strands on the other. If it looks as though you are getting the ends in a tangle, pull a single strand out of the mess and it will untangle. If you stop plaiting use a clothes peg to hold the last crossover to prevent the rest unravelling.
• Create interesting effects by mixing colours in the plaits. Use more than three strands – any multiple of three will do – or even plait three finished plaits together.

Weaving around a fork

To make simple yet effective embellishments, use a fork as a weaving loom.

1 Take a metal fork and a length of ribbon. Thread the ribbon through the middle hole in the fork, leaving a 5-cm tail to prevent unravelling.

2 Thread the ribbon alternately over and under the prongs of the fork. Keep weaving over and under the prongs until you have 8–10 rows of ribbon. Pull the two ends of ribbon tight so that the columns sit snugly together. Knot the ends.

3 Cut another length of ribbon and thread this through at the centre, at the base of the prongs. Wrap it around the weaving and over the top of the fork. Pull tight and hold the two ends together close to the weaving to gather and trap the weaving. Slide the ribbon off the fork in one swift motion to prevent unravelling.

4 Tighten the the length of ribbon so that the weaving forms a cylinder, then pull the ribbon ends tight and knot to hold in place. Fan out the loops or petals around the knotted ribbon to make a flower shape. Glue a contrast colour bead to the centre of the flower to finish.

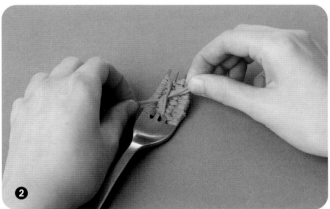

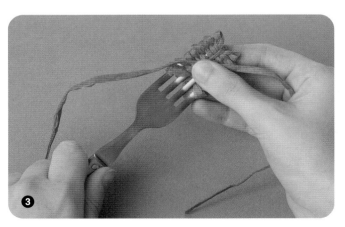

Japanese tray

This lacquered tray is inspired by traditional Japanese craftsmanship. The tray handle is made from kooboo cane, a type of rattan. The design is completed with a beaded tassel.

YOU WILL NEED:

- five 42 x 30 cm sheets of white construction paper (this is a type of cartridge paper often sold for children's crafts)
- craft knife
- metal ruler
- small tin of Japanese lacquer
- medium-sized paintbrush
- hole punch to make a hole that snugly fits the cane
- 2.3 m of 6-mm-wide kooboo cane (or use rattan or willow withies)
- strong black sewing thread
- Chinese lacquer bead tassel

1 Cut the paper into 5-cm-wide strips. You'll need about 36. Score each strip along its length with a craft knife 1 cm from one edge and 2 cm from the other edge. Fold each strip down the score lines with the largest flap on top. The finished strip is 2 cm wide.

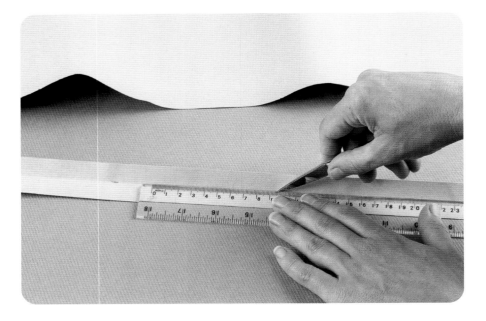

2 Weave the folded paper strips together, with 18 running vertically and 18 running horizontally to make a panel about 36-cm square. Adjust the weave if necessary so that the strips are equally spaced and at neat right angles to each other.

3 Turn the woven mat over. Leaving the corner strips aside, fold over every second strip along the edges of the mat and tuck in under the weave. Tuck in the alternating strips over the weave; this will leave the sides straight. Fold the corner strips over 1 cm beyond the side edges to create small tabs and tuck the ends into the weave. Trim off excess paper.

4 Turn the mat back over and paint with two coats of lacquer. Punch a hole in each corner the same diameter as the kooboo cane. Cut two pieces of kooboo cane 115 cm long and soak in water for about 30 minutes. Bend each piece in half and secure the ends together until dry. Feed the ends of the cane through the holes in the mat. To prevent the paper part of the tray from slipping down the 'legs', wrap black thread around the canes about 7 cm from the ends and tie off securely.

5 Tie the Japanese tassel embellishment in place at the point where the canes cross over as your final decoration. Your tray is now finished.

Weaving tip
Thick, expensive paper is too inflexible for this project. Construction paper is more easily woven together, and will crease well to make the crisply edged strips.

Woven basket

Fine paper string has been woven over cardboard to make this delightful basket. It is made in subtle neutral colours but you could use whatever suits your decor.

YOU WILL NEED:

- single-wall corrugated cardboard
- two skeins of paper string in five different colours
- two skeins of flat dark-brown coloured paper yarn
- pencil
- metal ruler
- craft knife
- cutting mat
- brown paper or brown paper bag
- tapestry needle

1 Enlarge the template on page 184 and cut the shape out of the corrugated cardboard. Measure and mark one of the large panels in the template to divide it into 10 equal sections. Measure 3 mm on either side of each line for the slits. Lay the template over the cardboard shape and mark the top and bottom of the slits with the point of a craft knife.

2 Score the cardboard shape to mark the base of the basket. Cut out the slits up to the score line. Mark and cut the slits on the other large panel. Turn the template around and position it centrally on one of the end panels. Mark and cut the slits in the same way.

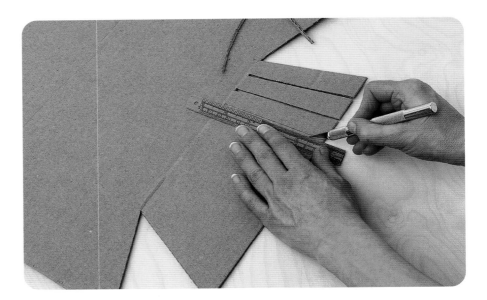

3 Beginning in one corner, weave a skein of coloured string over and under the card strips. When you get back to the first corner, wrap the skein round the tail end and start weaving in the opposite direction. As you weave, the sides of the basket will automatically stand up. Finish the skein in the corner where you began, leaving a tail on the inside. Begin a second colour, weaving around and back in the same way. Tie the two colours together in a secure knot and trim the ends neatly. Add more colours in the same way. Aim to keep the weaving level, but if necessary this can be corrected once the weaving is complete.

4 Stop weaving about 1 cm from the top. Cut 1-cm-wide strips from brown paper. Fold a strip over the top edge of the basket all around. Use paper yarn to oversew the top edge (enclosing the brown paper) and sew in the ends to finish.

Weaving tip

Cut out part of the template and weave a small sample piece to check the width of slit required between the sections for your particular string. The slits should remain the same width once woven. If the string doesn't fit neatly you need to adjust the size of the slits.

Mag bag

Take a page out of the latest style magazine and weave up this sturdy little bag — it's the perfect size to carry all your essentials. If you weave the strips carefully you can create little picture windows.

YOU WILL NEED:

- old fashion magazines
- clear sticky tape
- clothes pegs
- hot glue gun and glue sticks
- clear adhesive plastic sheet approximately 48 x 60 cm wide
- bamboo handbag handles
- darning needle and thread

1 Tear 36 pages from a magazine. Take one and fold it in half then in half again and again to create a thin strip. Make sure the torn edge is hidden. Make 36 folded strips.

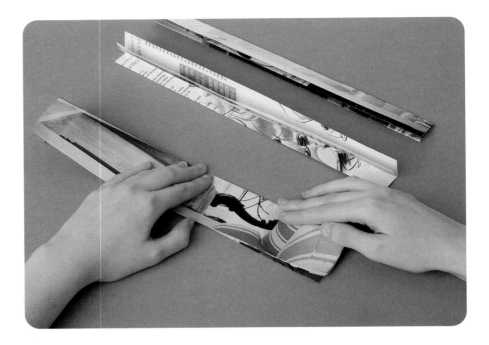

2 Slip one strip inside another and tape over the join. Repeat, joining the strips in pairs until you have 18 long strips altogether.

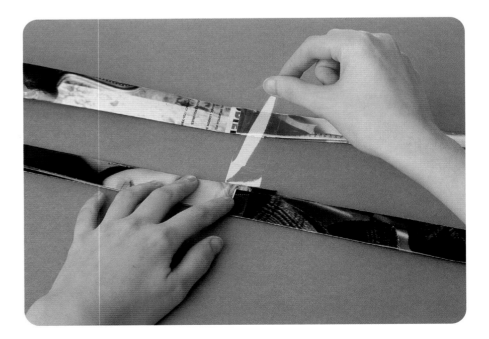

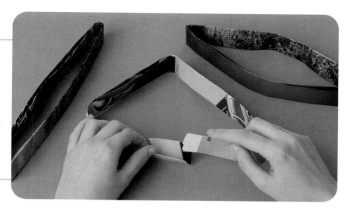

3 Take nine of the strips. On each strip put one end inside the other, as shown right, and tape over the join to create a loop or band. Leave the other nine strips long.

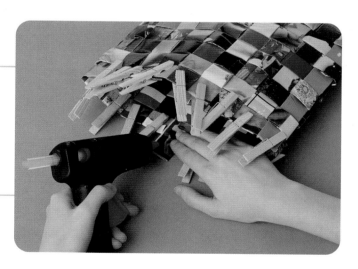

4 Put the nine bands alongside each other. Using one of the long strands, weave into the loop of the first band and over the next. The first band is the top rim of the bag, the band furthest away will be the bag bottom. Once you reach the last band, turn the whole set over and work the rest of the strip in and out of the bands on the back (you will put the strip through the second band up from the bottom first.) Use clothes pegs to secure the long strip (this forms one side of the bag).

5 Keep weaving until there is no more space and all the strips have been used. Turn over the ends and glue to the inside of the bag using the hot glue gun to give a strong bond.

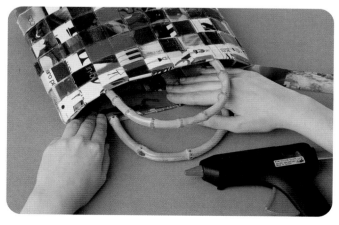

6 Cover the outside of the bag with the clear adhesive plastic sheet to waterproof it. Glue the handles to the inside of the bag using the hot glue gun and then stitch through the hole in the handles for added strength. Glue another folded strip of paper inside to cover the joins and base of the handles.

Plaited cocktail glass

Take inspiration from the colours and pizzazz of your favourite cocktail to stir up an exotic glass holder. Use them for summer drinks or make a set to keep your latte warm during the cooler months.

YOU WILL NEED:

- orange paper ribbon
- bright pink paper ribbon
- coloured wooden beads
- scissors
- hot glue gun and glue sticks
- orange thread and needle
- reusable adhesive putty
- fork

1 Cut the ribbon into 3-m lengths to plait together. Cut three orange and three pink lengths. Arrange them in pairs: two orange, two pink and one pink and orange pair.

2 Plait the lengths together (see page 130). When you reach the end, trim off any uneven strands and use a hot glue gun to stick the strands together. Start coiling the end around itself.

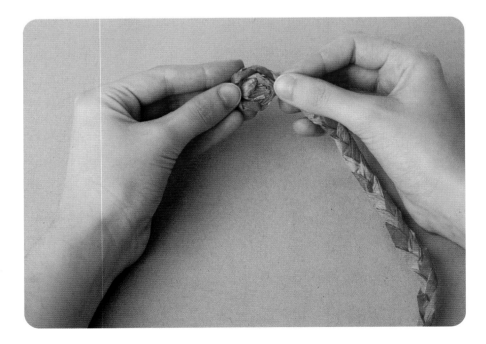

3   Thread a needle with orange thread and begin stitching around the glued end of the plait to make a base. Stitch on round the end, coiling the plait as you go.

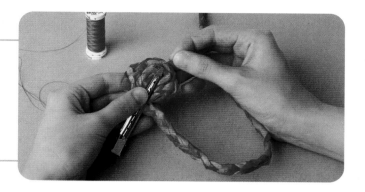

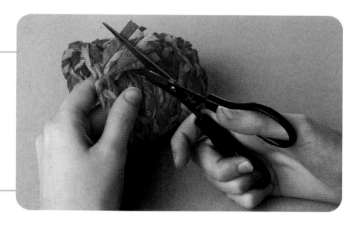

4   When the base is big enough to cover the bottom of the glass, put a blob of reusable adhesive putty on the base of the glass and press the coil on top. Turn the glass so that the rim is on the table top. Continue coiling and stitching the plait tightly around the cup.

5   When you reach the end of the plat trim away any excess ribbon and stitch the end down firmly. Turn the cup the other way out so that the stitches are now on the inside.

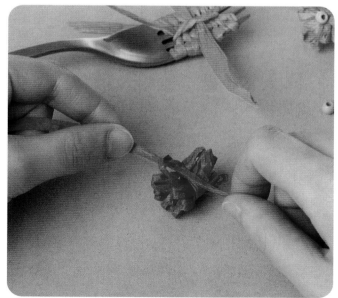

6   Make decorative flowers by winding more paper ribbon around a fork (see page 131). Leave tails on the back of each flower. Glue a coloured wooden bead to the centre of each flower using your hot glue gun. Thread the tails through the spaces in the stitching at the top of the holder and knot the tails inside to secure the flowers.

Coaster
Try making a coaster by coiling a plait flat and stitching it together. Simply extend the length of the plait to make a set of dinner mats.

PAPIER MÂCHÉ

Papier mâché has grown into a unique and exciting technique for contemporary papercrafters. A vast range of papers have reinvigorated the craft and taken it to new heights. Once you have a basic knowledge of the techniques and methods involved, you will be able to experiment with moulds and paste types to develop a range of effects from feathering to translucence and amazing three-dimensional projects.

Glue

PVA glue is the most common adhesive used for papier mâché. To achieve the best strength of solution, place 1 part PVA glue in a bowl and add 5 parts water. Mix together using an old paintbrush or stirring stick. The solution is ready to use immediately, and can be successfully stored in an airtight container or glass jar.

Flour paste

To make this traditional flour and water paste, bring 5 cups of water to the boil in a saucepan. Meanwhile, sieve a quarter of a cup of flour into some cold water and blend to a thick paste. When completely smooth, add the paste to the boiling water and stir for 2 minutes. Allow to cool, producing a runny glue that is ready to use straight away. Store for a maximum of a few days in an airtight container in the fridge.

Wallpaper paste

This is the perfect paste for larger projects. Follow the manufacturer's instructions to make up a glutinous paste. It will keep for a few days if stored in an airtight container in the fridge, just like flour paste.

Storing paste solution
Be sure to label any paste solution very clearly and always store in a suitable container out of the reach of children or animals.

Coloured paste

To jazz up an adhesive solution, add a splash of colour, sparkle or texture. Try mixing in a drop of poster paint, which will lightly tint white tissue paper projects. For a truly individual effect, add glitter, coloured sand or confetti pieces to the glue applied on the final coat.

Moulding tip
Try using discarded cardboard tubes, empty bottles, plastic cups and unusually shaped balloons as moulds for papier mâché.

Suitable paper

For more daring crafters there are a number of interesting paper options, such as handmade or Japanese paper, available from art suppliers and specialized stationers. Handmade paper comes in so many different varieties, from the very fine Japanese lace papers, which are ideal for creating a layer of texture, to thicker paper types, and papers made with flower petals, coloured chips and fibres. Some handmade papers will not be suitable for papier mâché, so always try them out first – heavy papers will not stick together while very thin or poor quality paper may disintegrate.

Most types of paper can be combined with other papers so you use your best papers over a base of newspaper, for example. Tissue paper is a source of inspiration for papier mâché as it works well when mixed with textured pastes and decorative paper.

Newsprint is cheap and readily available. It is easy to paint over the text after the paper has dried. When using newsprint, tissue, origami or heavy handmade paper, tear the paper with the grain into strips, then again to form squares. This method has been used to tear the mesh-style paper shown below. You may need to cut rather than tear lace paper or other papers with no obvious grain.

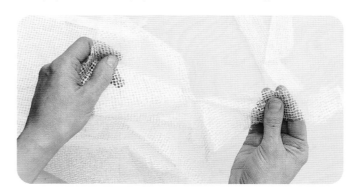

Moulding with paper

Paper can be moulded in strips or left to soak and formed into a pulp. Almost any object can be used as a mould. Just make sure that the shape is wider at the top than at the bottom so that the finished project can be lifted out easily without being damaged.

If you are using a plastic mould, coat it with petroleum jelly, olive oil or washing-up liquid, so that once the paper

has dried it can be easily removed. For more solid types of mould such as metal or ceramic bowls, use non-stick foil or plastic food wrap to cover the mould and apply the layers of paper. Once the papier mâché has dried, pull the sides of foil or food wrap so that the papier mâché is released from the mould, then peel away and discard.

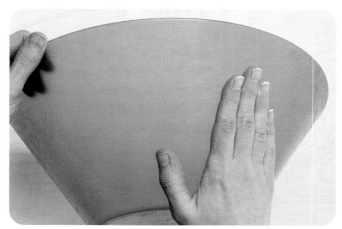

❶ Smear a plastic bowl with petroleum jelly, olive oil or washing-up liquid to prevent the paper from sticking.

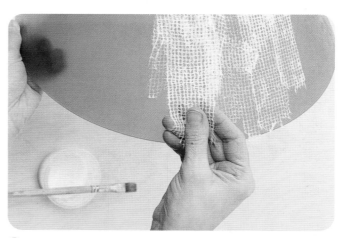

❷ Paste paper onto the mould piece by piece, using your glue or paste solution and an old paintbrush.

Wire moulding

Many crafters are put off using wire because of the sharp edges, which make it a more dangerous technique. However, as long as you are careful, this can be a wonderful material to use, as it avoids having to find a mould of the right size for your project. Another advantage is that if the mould becomes a part of the project it does not have to be removed afterward. Mould a simple shape and cover in paper, adding any details afterward. This is a good method if you want to use paper pulp as you can press it around the wire.

Paper pulp

Tear paper into 8-cm squares, place them in a bowl and soak in water overnight. In the morning, push the paper through a sieve to drain away the excess water and to aid the pulping process. Mix the pulp with some PVA glue to bind the pulp together. The mixture is ready to be used immediately – do not try to store it.

Use paper pulp to form into shapes such as beads or cast it into picture frames or other forms. You can even shape it around different types of mould or wire-mesh shapes or use it in conjunction with paper strips to create special features such as mouldings.

Using balloons

Balloons can be used to make simple bowl or vase shapes. Blow up a balloon, and cover it with layers of paper and glue solution. To begin, work around the equator of the balloon, then fill in half of the balloon, leaving the knotted end of the balloon unpasted. Add 2–3 layers then leave it to dry overnight. The next day try adding small pieces of origami paper as a final layer and some glitter glue. Leave the work to dry overnight once more.

Once dry, carefully pop the balloon with a needle or pair of scissors – it should come away very easily from papier mâché. If you want to give the bowl a base, add longer strips widthways across the bottom. Flatten and straighten the base by placing your paper bowl upright and pushing down on the base from the inside.

Two-colour bowls

These bowls have any number of possible uses especially if you protect them with matt varnish. Most styles of bowl can be used as a mould, as long as the shape is wider at the top than at the bottom.

YOU WILL NEED:

- large shallow bowl to use as a mould
- non-stick aluminium foil
- PVA glue (white craft glue)
- large sheet of rhododendron-coloured handmade paper
- small sponge
- large sheet of natural-coloured handmade mulberry paper

1 Cover the bowl with aluminium foil, smoothing the foil until it is as flat as possible. Dilute the PVA glue with 5 parts water. Roughly tear the rhododendron-coloured paper into 2.5 to 5 cm pieces.

2 Using the sponge, cover the paper with the diluted glue solution and paste the pieces on top of the foil. Keep adding the paper until the entire bowl is covered with two layers. Leave the top edge fairly ragged. Allow to dry overnight, away from direct heat.

3 Once dry, cover the papier mâché with several layers of natural-coloured mulberry paper. You may need to make several layers before the dye stops seeping through the mulberry paper. Allow the glue to dry between the extra layers. (Don't rush this.)

Coating tip

If you are using a plastic bowl as a mould, do not cover it with foil. Instead, smear it with a thin coat of petroleum jelly or olive oil before you start.

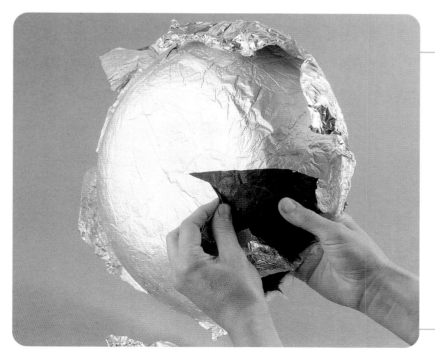

4 Leave the finished bowl to dry overnight. Once the papier mâché is dry, lift it carefully out of the bowl and peel off the aluminium foil. Cover the outside of the bowl with another layer of rhododendron-coloured paper and allow to dry, balanced upside down. Don't trim the edges too much – these are deliberately left rough for a delicate, feathered effect to reveal the contrasting colours.

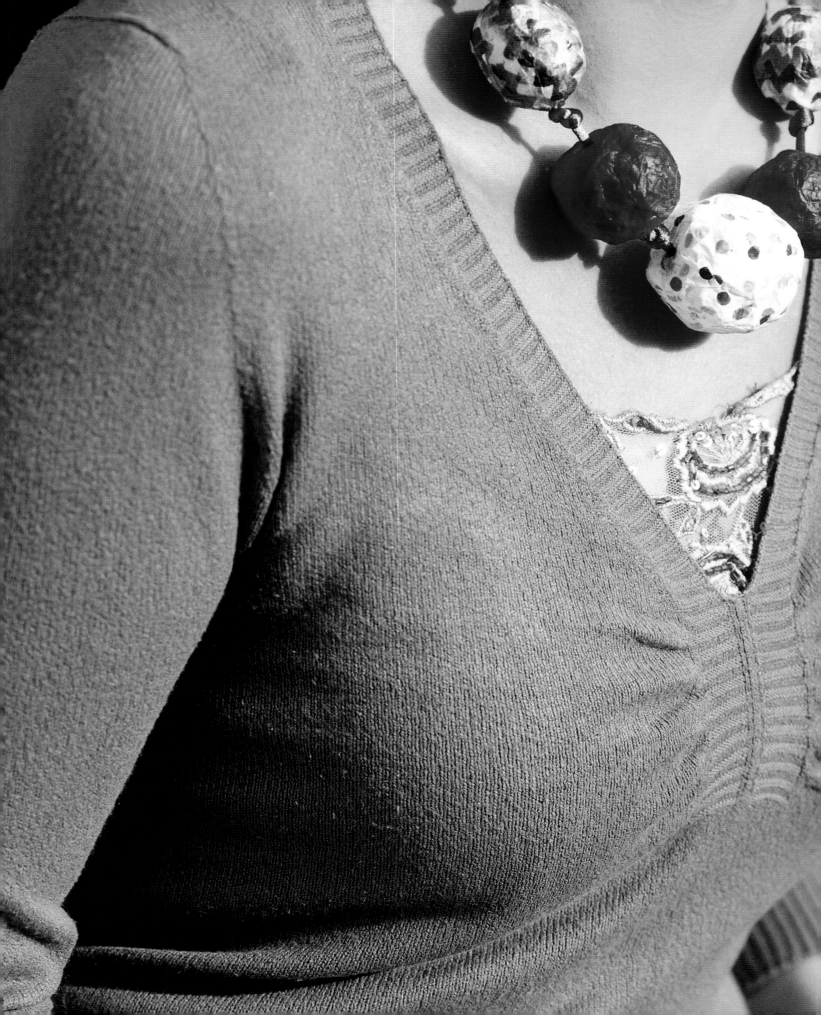

Big beads necklace

Show off your papercrafting skills with this funky necklace. Choose densely patterned tissue paper to achieve the best effects, and use a good-quality clasp and pure silk cord to set off your work.

YOU WILL NEED:

- white paper pulp (see page 151) or white tissue and glue solution (see page 149)
- various colours/patterns of coordinating tissue paper
- cocktail sticks
- various sizes and shapes of wooden beads
- paste brush or old paintbrush
- low-tack sticky tape
- 1 m of purple silk cord
- darning needle
- necklace clasp suitable for use with the cord (optional)

1 Place a cocktail stick through the middle of a wooden bead. This gives you something to hold while you are adding the paper layers and ensures that the hole is not covered over. Add a layer of white paper pulp or tissue paper strips applied with glue to the bead.

2 Keep compressing more pulp or layers of tissue around the bead to build up the size you require (a variety of sizes are used here). You can also mould the shape around a cocktail stick without using a bead to create a variety of beads of your choice. Leave to dry for a few hours, preferably not overnight (the beads should not dry completely).

3 Once the beads are nearly dry begin to add strips of the patterned tissue paper, layering on the strips with a glue solution and a paste brush or old paintbrush. Using some of the plain tissue paper, create plain beads to coordinate with the patterned beads. Leave all the beads to dry thoroughly for at least 24 hours.

4 Wrap some low-tack sticky tape around the cord to protect one end and act as a needle. Tie an overhand knot at other end of the cord at least 20 cm from the end. This will be the position of the first bead. Thread on the first bead and tie another knot behind it, using a needle to slip the knot down close to the bead. Add the beads in series, knotting between each one and after the last one. Trim the ends of the necklace cord to fit. You can simply tie the cord at the back of the neck with a neat bow, or add a pretty clasp.

Leafy cups

These gorgeous translucent vases will let the light shine through – try them on a windowsill for maximum effect. Make smaller versions to hold a glass for a small candle to create a romantic setting.

- white tissue paper
- coloured Japanese lace paper or similar
- clear plastic cup
- scissors
- PVA glue
- old paintbrush or paste brush to apply the glue
- dried leaves to coordinate with the colour of the Japanese lace paper

Do not leave lit candles unattended. Put the candles in a glass container before you put them inside the plastic vase. The sides of the glass container should exceed the height of the vase.

1 If the cup has a rim, cut it off carefully to the approximate height of your choice. Tear up the white tissue paper and cut the lace paper into rough 8-cm squares. Make up a glue solution of 1 part PVA glue and 5 parts water, mixing it well.

2 With an old paintbrush or paste brush, paint some glue onto each tissue paper square and layer onto the inside of the cup. To secure each square, paint a further coat of glue solution on top of the paper. Repeat the process with more squares until the inside of the glass is covered with 1 to 3 randomly placed layers of tissue.

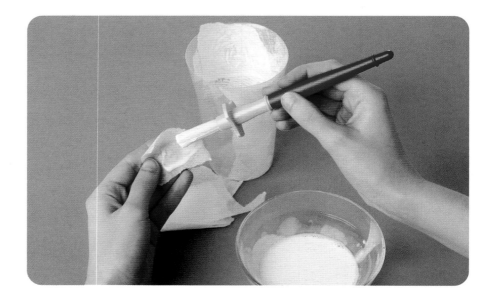

3 Now begin placing the paper on the outside of the cup, starting with the tissue paper. Repeat the process using the lace paper, placing the pieces neatly this time.

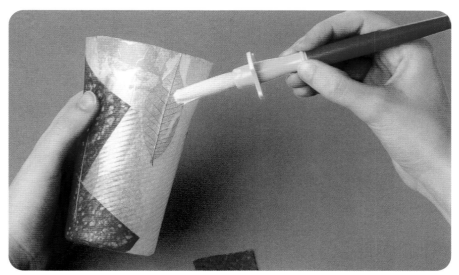

4 While adding the lace paper, add occasional dried leaves, trapping them between the layers of paper.

5 Once the cup is completely dry, neatly trim the edges at the top. For an eye-catching effect, place one final square diagonally on the cup or add a leaf or two.

Embellishment
Experiment with different papers and embellishments, such as feathers, small buttons or gems.

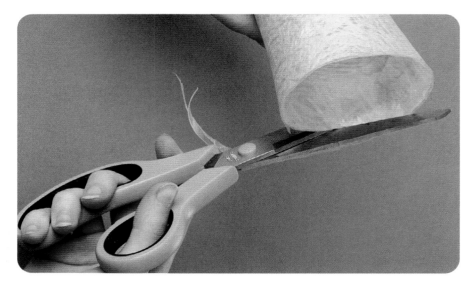

STITCHING

Stitching can be applied to paper just as easily as it can be applied to fabrics. Stitches range from the elaborate freestyle embroidery to simple backstitch and running stitch, which are suited to attaching paper to cards. For basic stitching a needle and thread will suffice, although a sewing machine can also give pleasing results.

Hand embroidery

Backstitches can be used alongside other stitches or on their own to create outline pictures. They resemble running stitch, but form a continuous line. The stitch is made by inserting the needle from the back of the fabric or paper and then inserting it back down one space behind or in the previous hole – this will give a continuous line.

Long stitches are a lovely variation and can be less uniform in size. Here the stitch is used to create the flower stems. You could also try chain stitch or working french knots (as shown on the left) to create more extravagant stitching.

Cross-stitch

Cross-stitches are made up of two diagonal lines that cross over each other, and are traditionally used on fabric such as linen and Aida, and more recently on plastic canvas or perforated paper. The holes are uniformly spaced so that neat even stitches are achieved. In cross-stitch it is important to remember that all the top stitches should lie in the same direction. Basic cross-stitches can be used randomly spaced to embellish paper, or in each of the four corners of a piece of paper to attach it to another piece. Try using this stitch to create a snow scene with white thread on a dark-coloured piece of paper.

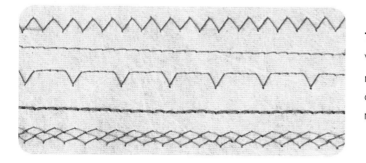

Using a sewing machine

Various stitches can be added to paper with a sewing machine. Zigzag and straight stitch are probably the most commonly used machine stitches in papercraft, although most modern machines can also work embroidery stitches.

Sewing with ribbon

Ribbon embroidery is made by threading a large-holed needle with very narrow ribbon and making simple stitches. A craft in its own right, the technique produces beautiful results on both fabric and paper. You don't need to use complicated stitches when using ribbon. Long stitches, French knots and lazy-daisy stitch all work extremely well.

Stitching on paper

Stitching on paper can produce some really pleasing effects. The stitches can be used simply to attach papers together or to make pockets and borders. Plain stitches such as running stitch and machine zigzag will work well on most occasions.

When stitching on paper by hand it is important to make the holes first. This helps to plan where the stitches are going to go and makes the stitching easier, especially if thick paper is used. You may wish to mark an outline in pencil to help guide you. Place the paper on a suitable mat and, using a needle or specially made pricking tool, make evenly spaced holes along the outline. Once all the holes have been made, thread a needle and start stitching.

Different effects can be achieved by replacing stranded cotton or machine thread with metallic or pearl threads, ribbon or yarn. When stitching with a sewing machine, there is no need to make holes in the paper first.

Using templates

There are a number of specialist templates available for papercrafts. Some are multi-templates and contain an embossing pattern, pricking, and cutting pattern as well as areas to stitch. These can make easy yet unusual and stunning cards. Long running stitches are generally used with these templates, but you can use any stitches you like, even a series of French knots to create an unusual three-dimensional effect.

Beads and buttons

Additional trimmings such as beads and buttons can really bring stitched projects to life. They can be combined with other craft techniques such as rubber stamping to make truly unique items. Buttons and beads are attached to paper or fabric using small stitches.

Spirelli and lacing

There is a paper and thread art form called spirelli or spirella, which involves winding thread around special card forms to produce all sorts of beautiful designs. The card shapes have scalloped edges that hold the thread in place in the grooves. Different designs are produced by winding the thread in different ways. You can produce your own shapes by cutting simple forms out of card with scalloped-edge or pinking shears. Alternatively, pierce holes around the edge of your card shape and pass the thread between the holes, as shown here.

Stitching around motifs

Stitching around motifs on patterned paper can have a pleasing effect that looks rather like appliqué. Some patterns will look better than others, so experiment with different weights of paper and designs. The effect can be made more decorative by stitching with metallic thread or adding tiny beads.

Stitching onto fabric

When stitching on fabric, fray the edges before mounting the work to achieve a natural finish. Treat the edges with specialist anti-fraying products if you wish to keep material edges straight without hemming or sewing the edges under. Stitched fabric pieces can be added to cards and other papercraft items by stitching them on or using a dry adhesive.

Fabric with holes

The easiest way to make a stitched picture is by using perforated paper or evenweave fabric.

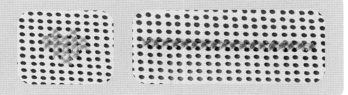

Tucked lampshade

This calming lampshade is made from strengthened tissue paper,
which can be handled like fabric, dyed and stitched without tearing.
The elegant rippling pattern softens the light passing through.

YOU WILL NEED:

- white drum lampshade 21 cm high and 28 cm in diameter
- three 55 x 80 cm sheets of strong white tissue paper
- mint-green dye (or colour of your choice)
- newspaper
- sponge brush
- scissors
- sewing machine
- mint-green thread
- double-sided sticky tape
- self-adhesive white paper tape

1 Mix the dye with water to make a dye solution, following the manufacturer's instructions. Lay each sheet of tissue paper on several layers of newspaper and brush with the dye solution. Lift onto fresh newspaper and allow to dry flat.

2 Cut each sheet of tissue paper in half lengthways. Mark every 2.5 cm down each long side. Fold the paper between the first two marks and flatten the crease with your finger.

3 Using the side of the presser foot as a guide, machine stitch approximately 1 cm from the fold. Fold the paper between the next two marks and stitch a second tuck in place. The fold of this tuck should touch the stitching of the first. Continue folding and stitching until the entire panel is complete. Make five panels in total. With right sides together, stitch the panels together along the short edges, maintaining an even distance between the tucks.

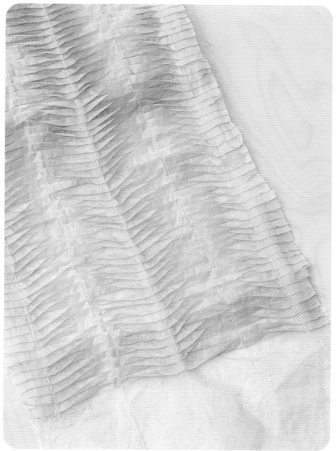

4 Trim the seam allowance to 5 mm and press with a cool iron. Press the tucks in the same direction. Fold the panel in half lengthways. Mark every 5 cm out from the central fold along the short edges of the panel. Fold the panel between the marks; you should have five lengthways creases. Machine stitch down the central fold in the direction of the tucks. Stitch both outer creases in the same direction. Turn the panel around and line up one of the remaining creases under the presser foot. Lift the first few tucks, fold over and stitch flat. Continue lifting a few tucks and stitching down in the opposite direction to form a zigzag effect. Repeat on the remaining crease.

Trim the threads close to the paper. Attach the stitched paper to the shade with thin strips of double-sided tape around the top and bottom rim and down the back seam. In order to keep the tucks vertical, attach around the bottom of the shade first then ease the top edge and press onto the double-sided tape. Trim the top and bottom edge of the stitched panel to 1 cm. Fold to the inside of the lampshade and cover the raw edges neatly with white paper tape .

Handmade card

This lovely card looks very complicated but it isn't difficult to make — if sewing is a problem, use dimensional paint instead. Choosing papers and embellishments in several shades of one colour assures success.

YOU WILL NEED:

- two 21 x 30 cm sheets of cream card
- three handmade papers at least 18 x 14 cm in coordinating designs
- 1 piece of sparkly paper measuring 8 x 12.5 cm
- scissors or craft knife and cutting mat
- bone folder
- double-sided sticky tape
- embroidery needle
- silver stranded embroidery thread
- three porcelain flower buttons

1 Cut a 15 x 21 cm rectangle of cream card, and score and fold it in half widthways to make the basic card (which will fit in a 11.5 x 16 cm envelope). Use a bone folder to smooth the fold (see page 58).

2 Cut four 3.5 x 5.5 cm rectangles from your two lightest coloured handmade papers. Cut a 6.5 x 11 cm rectangle of cream card and use double-sided tape to stick the rectangles of handmade paper on top so that they meet at the middle. Trim off any excess around the edges. Cut a heart shape from deeper coloured textured paper to fit neatly on the card.

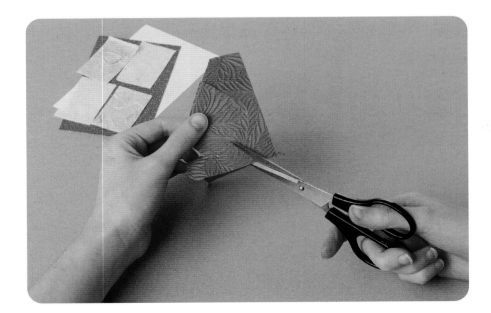

3 Stick the heart onto the centre of the rectangle where the four handmade papers meet. Use hand or machine zigzag stitches to attach the heart to the card. If you are using a machine, make sure your stitches are not too close together or they will tear or cut the paper. Stitch around the edge of the card with backstitch or running stitch.

4 Stick the heart card onto the rectangle of sparkly paper. Mount it onto a slightly larger piece of cream card and then finally onto a piece of one of the handmade papers. Stick the finished rectangle centrally on the front of the folded card. Stick or sew the porcelain flower embellishments to the centre of the heart.

Hand stitching

If you are stitching the card by hand, remember to make holes for the stitches first. You may find a faint pencil outline helps to guide you.

Ivy table set

These simple yet stylish table decorations can be used all year round.

Stitching the leaves together gives a fantastic three-dimensional effect.

Wrap the leaves around a vase to make a more traditional centrepiece.

YOU WILL NEED:

- assortment of origami papers in contrasting patterns and coordinating colours
- white leather thong: 120 cm for the runner and 60 cm for each napkin ring
- soft pencil
- scissors
- sewing needle
- sewing thread to coordinate with the origami papers

For a table runner and four napkin rings you will need 3.6 m of leather thong.

1 Trace the ivy leaf templates below, then enlarge to double the size on a photocopier. Trace the designs onto an assortment of origami papers. For the table runner, you will need five of template 1, eight of template 2, four of template 3, seven of template 4, and five of template 5.

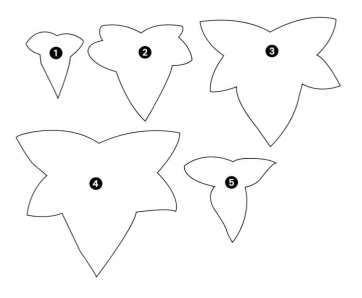

2 Fold all the leaves in half to make a crease line, then unfold. Group the leaves in sets of two and three layers of leaves in decreasing sizes, with a mixture of contrasting patterns.

3 Lay out the leather thong for the runner flat on a table. Position the groups of leaves along the thong until you are pleased with the effect. Once you are happy with the arrangement, stitch the layers of leaves in place. Make two or three stitches down the centre crease through all the layers of paper in each group of leaves.

Cutting tip
Use decorative edging shears to cut some of the leaves for added interest.

4 Take the thread behind the leaf, wrap it around the leather thong and tie in place. This allows the position of the leaves to be adjusted. Re-crease the folds for a more three-dimensional effect. Repeat steps 1–4 to make a napkin ring, using 60 cm of thong and three different leaf shapes per ring.

Stitched corsages

Thick handmade papers, especially those with a high cotton content, can be stitched in the same way as felt and embellished with beads and sequins. Here the idea is used to make lovely flower brooches.

YOU WILL NEED:

- yellow and orange chunky handmade paper, preferably with a high cotton content
- soft pencil
- scissors
- needle and threads (to match the paper colours)
- yellow sequins
- small gold beads
- big red bead for each flower
- 8 red medium-sized faceted beads
- brooch fitting for each flower

1 Make a flower template with curved or pointed petals, using the template on page 185, if desired. Draw around it onto yellow and orange paper so you have two flowers. Cut them out.

2 Thread a needle and knot the end well. Around the centre of each flower work about four running stitches. Pull them tight to gather the centre then knot your thread on the back.

3 Thread a needle with yellow thread and begin stitching the yellow flower. Come through to the front and thread on a sequin followed by a gold bead. Stitch back through the hole in the sequin and paper. Come back to the front and continue stitching on sequins, securing each one with a bead at the centre.

4 When the flower is full of sequins and beads, knot your thread on the back and trim the thread ends. Place the yellow flower on top of the orange flower. (Add more flower shapes at this point, as desired). Thread a needle and stitch through the centre from the back. Come up to the centre of the yellow flower and slide on a red bead. Stitch back through several times to join the flower together and secure the bead.

5 Come out through a hole in the bead. Thread on eight faceted smaller red beads and then stitch through the big bead again so the smaller beads form a ring around the central bead. Secure the smaller beads with a few stitches. Stitch a brooch fitting onto the reverse of the flower.

Colour tip
To soften the colours of the papers and create a natural gradation of colour you can dab on a weak bleach solution before you stitch and assemble the flowers. Always wear protective clothing when using bleach.

TEMPLATES

Right: Woven basket template, see page 138. Enlarge to the desired size using a photocopier. The dotted lines form the base of the box.

Below: Christmas box templates, see page 94. Enlarge both templates on the same scale to fit your box. Repeat the pattern by moving the template along to the left or right of the first tracing and sometimes flipping it over.

Top: Corsage template, see page 182. Make two copies, one slightly larger for the background layer.
Above: Flower ball template, see page 54.

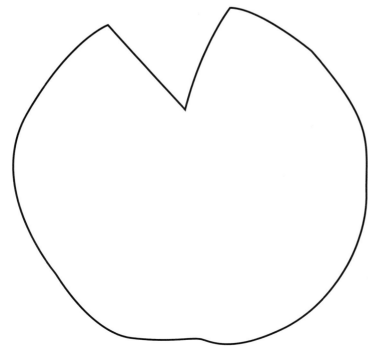

Above and left: Water lily and pad templates, see page 86.
Use a photocopier to enlarge the templates, as desired.

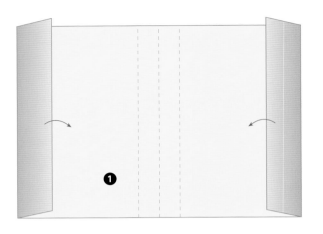

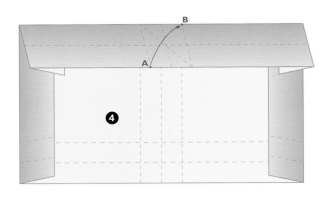

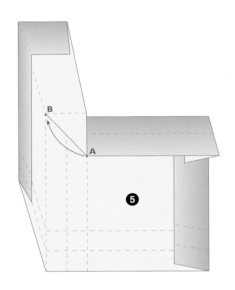

Above: Folding diagrams, see page 63.
Below: Punched border template, see page 82. Enlarge the template to the desired depth. Repeat the pattern by sliding the template to the left or right of your first tracing.

Left: Japanese hanging, see page 90. Enlarge the squares to the desired size, making sure each square is enlarged to the same scale.

Below: Mexican style candles, see page 78. Enlarge this template to fit the circumference of your candles, or use it to inspire your own designs.

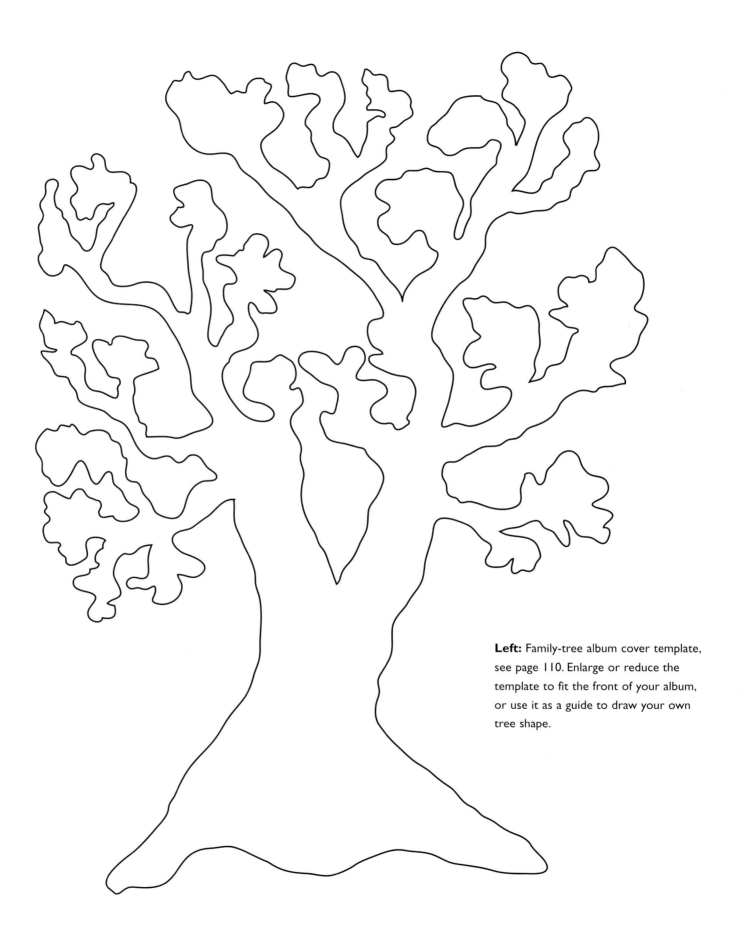

Left: Family-tree album cover template, see page 110. Enlarge or reduce the template to fit the front of your album, or use it as a guide to draw your own tree shape.

ACKNOWLEDGEMENTS

The makers:

Grateful thanks to all the wonderful designers involved with the book who were willing to take the art of papercraft to new heights.

Emma Angel
Text on pages 56–9, 72–5, 112–5, 128–31.
Origami picture frames on pages 64–7
Travel journal on pages 68–71
Water lilies on pages 84–7
Quilled box lid on pages 116–19
Rock-and-roll cuff on pages 120–3
Holiday wreath on pages 124–7
Mag bag on pages 140–3
Plaited cocktail glasses 144–7
Stitched corsages 180–3

Joanne Sanderson
Text on pages 10–37, 40–3, 97–9, 164–7.
Writing set on pages 44–7
Scented flower ball on pages 52–5
Jewellery box on pages 104–7
Family-tree album 108–11
Handmade card 172–5

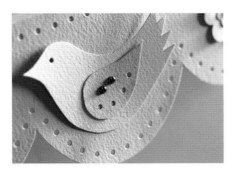

Dorothy Wood
Special thanks for putting together the original proposal, and for supplying so much help and inspiration through the project.
Gift tags 48–51
Pressed flower gift bags on pages 60–3
Shelf border on pages 80–3
Japanese hanging on pages 88–91
Japanese vases on pages 100–103
Japanese tray on pages 132–5
Woven basket on pages 136–9
Two-colour bowls on pages 152–5
Tucked and stitched lampshade on pages 168–71

Lucie Pritchard
Text on pages 148–51.
Big beads necklace on pages 156–9
Leafy cups on pages 160–3

Kim Robertson
Christmas box on pages 92–5
Ivy table runner on pages 176–9

Karin Hossack
Mexican candles on pages 76–9

The stockists

A big thank-you to the following companies who loaned props for the shoot:

HobbyCraft
The Arts and Crafts Superstore
25 superstores, 32,000 products for 250 creative activities all under one roof. Store locations call
0800 027 2387
or visit www.hobbycraft.co.uk

An Angel at my Table (London) Ltd.
116A Fortress Road
London NW5 2HL
Tel: 0207 424 9777
Fax: 0207 424 9666
Email: londonshop@ angelatmytable.intervivo.com

Picture credits

Photography by Sian Irvine.
Additional Photography by Lucinda Symons on pages 48–51, 60–3, 72, 76–83, 88–91, 96, 100–3, 132–9, 148, 150, 152–5, 168–71.
Additional pictures supplied by:
Page 10 © Bob Krist/Corbis
Page 11 © Getty Images
Page 12 © Patrick Robert/ Sygma/CORBIS
Page 13 © Mary Evans Picture Library
Page 15 © Bihemian Nomad Picturemakers/CORBIS
Page 17 © Austrian Archives/CORBIS
Page 18 © Cynthia Hart Designer/CORBIS
Page 19 © Historical Picture Archive/CORBIS

INDEX